T0354060

The Elite Secretary

The Definitive Guide to a Successful Career

Sandra C. Rorbak

iUniverse, Inc.
Bloomington

The Elite Secretary
The Definitive Guide to a Successful Career

iUniverse books may be ordered through booksellers or by contacting:

iUniverse
1663 Liberty Drive
Bloomington, IN 47403
www.iuniverse.com
1-800-Authors (1-800-288-4677)

ISBN: 978-1-4697-9827-1 (sc)
ISBN: 978-1-4697-9828-8 (hc)
ISBN: 978-1-4697-9829-5 (e)

Library of Congress Control Number: 2012904624

Printed in the United States of America

iUniverse rev. date: 5/18/2012

To Sarah-Jane Mvemve Mavunga, my dearest mother, who passed away in May of 2009. Her passing would always have come too soon for me, but it is especially saddening that it came just two years before she could witness this, my proudest and greatest accomplishment. She sacrificed a great deal to ensure that each of her three children had the opportunity to get the best possible education. I hold dear the values of honesty, integrity, discipline, and hard work that she instilled in me as I continue to navigate through my own professional life.

~

To my darling departed husband, Knud Rorbak, without whom I might never have realized this dream.

No one can make you feel inferior without your consent.

—Eleanor Roosevelt

Contents

Preface

Some years ago I found myself reflecting on my long secretarial career and pondering the numerous probing questions I had fielded from young men and women who were interested in pursuing the same profession. As the questions turned into requests for advice, I was prompted to research the published works covering this topic in bookstores and my local library. I discovered that a number of gifted authors have provided insights into the work of a professional secretary. However, having worked as a secretary on three continents, I realised I had my own unique perspective to bring to the discussion. Granted, there are hundreds of publications about typing, transcribing, filing, and office automation, as well as guides on how to become a legal secretary and books about the role of administrative assistants. However, my intent in this book is to delve deeper and describe the real experiences that a new secretary is likely to encounter on the job and how best to handle sticky situations. Furthermore, I want to present my own account of the corporate world and that of the secretaries who contributed to this book as they and I have known it—the stuff that is often hidden between the lines, like a cryptic message—a realistic portrayal of "a day in the life of" and a behind-the-scenes look at the life of a secretary.

I must be clear from the outset that this isn't a naming-names, dish-the-dirt exposé. While I do elaborate extensively on actual experiences in this book that show the repercussions of such actions, they are presented as examples, and *no real names are cited*. In fact, rule number one for succeeding as a secretary is discretion, and it is crucial to remain well away from the lures of gossip mongering. A person who fails to follow these rules is unlikely ever to make it to the pinnacle of her career, as a secretary who cannot be trusted is doomed. Rule number two is to never, ever openly make disparaging remarks about current or former employers *by name*. This is bound to come back to haunt you one day.

My aim in writing this book is twofold: (a) to provide a how-to guide that is informative and educational, offering some real-life examples to anyone with an interest in pursuing a secretarial career, and (b) to provide practical tools and reminders for handling the ambiguous aspects of the job to those who have already embarked on their secretarial journey.

If I were starting out today and thinking about a secretarial career, I would want to know what I could truly expect in the wide world of corporate work life. If you ask this question to those who are already in the profession, you might not get a satisfactory response, because there are many secretaries working today who are as perplexed as ever by the political aspects of the job, which they often don't know how to solve. Turning to friends in the workplace may not help to resolve them either. Furthermore, there are those who, because of their frustration or unconscious surrender to intimidation, office politics, bullies, imperious bosses, discrimination, or power-play tactics, might be considering flight as the only way out of a bad situation. To those people I am here to say STOP! Hear me out. I have lived it. What you are going through happens to dozens of secretaries. You do not have to succumb to it—you need to learn how to play the game. There are life lessons to be learned from many trying situations. Taking flight only decelerates your learning process.

It is my hope that the secretary of the future will be viewed as an expert in her field, a consummate professional who persistently demonstrates the core competencies for success. While she might be labelled differently in the future, I hope her important role in the modern office is both recognized and appreciated.

Sandra C. Rorbak

Acknowledgments

I commenced writing this book in 2002, and the peaks and valleys of my life shaped its progress. I owe a debt of gratitude to my first editor, Patricia Anderson (Vancouver, Canada), for accepting the challenge of taking on the first raw manuscript of a novice writer and muddling through the process of not only helping me to find my writer's voice but also educating me on the nuances of writing for publication.

To the editor who guided me through the second phase of this book, my champion, my writing conscience, Mary Patricia Bishop (Toronto, Canada), I will be eternally grateful not only for the glistening wordsmithing but even more so for her words of encouragement and the skilful ways in which she challenged me to rethink and reword some of my bold statements. My genuine thanks to her for editing my manuscript without stifling or altering my voice.

Special thanks go to Shealah Stratton (Toronto, Canada) for her incredible patience and dedication to making my book ready for print. I am tremendously grateful for her insightful, meticulous approach to editing, which inspired me to strive to be a better writer. You are indeed a "good editor," if not one of the best.

To Andrea Wiwchar (Vancouver, Canada), thank you for your candour and kind contribution to this project. You always come through for me and for that I am grateful.

Finally, I wish to thank every secretary who was brave enough to lend his or her voice and experiences to this project, and to the managers and bosses who candidly expressed their positive and negative experiences with their own secretaries. I thank you for your honesty, and for the balance and gravitas you have added to this book.

List of Illustrations

Dear Reader,

More often than not the secretary of today is female, and because of this I have chosen to habitually refer to her as female. However, the reader is asked to remember that the reference should be regarded as a gender-neutral one. Similarly, in this book the boss is primarily referred to as male, but there are now as many female bosses as there are male ones.

Chapter 1:
Why Become a Secretary?

People choose the secretarial route for a variety of reasons. Many fall into the role by accident, others specifically set out to work in this field, and some use it as a starting point for climbing the corporate ladder. Whatever the reason, secretaries have been in existence since the establishment of the office and will undoubtedly continue to exist as long as there are offices and bosses.

If you are starting out today, in the twenty-first century, how do you decide if this is the right field for you, especially if you have no insight into the day-to-day challenges of the secretarial world? A career counsellor could certainly give you some guidance, and your secretarial training might illuminate some of the more ambiguous aspects of the job, but you would only be scratching the surface of what you need to know.

The minimal choices for women in past decades simplified the decision-making process, as social pressures dictated that a woman planning to join the professional ranks usually chose to become a teacher, nurse, or secretary. However, events in the late-twentieth century altered this scenario, and as a result gender demographics in the career landscape have drastically changed. Women are no longer so limited in their choice of a career.

In the course of writing this book, I researched the trends over the years in theory and in practice and discovered that the secretarial role of today is greatly expanded from that of earlier years. The expectations faced by those in the role are greater today than they were when I entered the profession some twenty years ago. Responsibilities and duties have evolved. I reviewed hundreds of recent job postings for administrative and executive assistants (the preferred job titles since the late 1990s), and the common thread in these advertisements was that they required experience in a particular industry. Employers have the prerogative to be specific because they know the role and the skill set that is required for the aspiring candidate to be successful.

The word "secretary" has been used less and less since the year 2000 because of the increased responsibility and ever-changing scope of the work. Hence some people take offense at being called a secretary, because in their view the label has the debasing connotation of the bubblegum-chewing airhead filing her nails while answering the phone. I would like to believe that as a society, we have moved on from this uninformed notion about secretaries. In fact, I presume that the enlightened members of our civilization appreciate the contributions personal secretaries have made to their ability to do their jobs. When I consulted with one senior executive about the merits of a good secretary, he unabashedly confessed to me that without his secretary at the helm of all his business dealings he would be lost, adding that she seamlessly organized his professional life. His final comment summed up his perception: "I absolutely respect and value her contribution to my company."

The reality of being a secretary is both more challenging and more appealing than most people realize. Secretaries must possess certain qualities in order to be successful in their field. These attributes are crucial and will be put to the test repeatedly in the workplace. Exhibiting some, if not all, of the following traits will propel a secretary to greatness:

- Approachable
- Astute
- Dependable
- Detail oriented
- Discreet
- Ethical
- Hard-working
- Honest
- Intelligent
- Loyal
- Knowledgeable
- Respectful

- Trustworthy

An important point to clarify, particularly at this stage of your decision-making process, is the subordinate nature of this role. Secretaries will forever work for and report to someone, commonly (or affectionately) referred to as "the boss." If your aspirations are to become your own boss some day while remaining in this role, you might need to rethink your decision. Secretaries may act as pseudo-managers, but this is limited to administrative work and their own job function. The nearest a secretary can ever come to having the title of "manager" is to be appointed office manager or office administration manager. This is a glorified version of an office administrator and refers to the person who manages the running of the office and its administrative processes. While it is true that some administrative personnel may report to the office manager, such as a filing clerk or office receptionist, this is not a high-level management position.

My advice for someone looking to embark on a secretarial career is to do your homework first. Your initial decision should be based on the industry in which you would like to specialize. The playing field is broad, ranging from the different levels of government to the diverse private sector, including real estate, engineering, the medical and legal professions, oil and gas, telecommunications, insurance, finance, banking, advertising, marketing, human resources, travel and tourism, communications, and entertainment. Job postings within any of these areas will often cite a minimum requirement of experience related to that industry.

Where do you start to look for direction prior to focusing on specific training in one area? Ideally, you will get all the necessary information about job prospects during the secretarial training period. If, however, you are still in high school and are curious about secretarial opportunities, I suggest visiting the careers sections of libraries and bookstores . Read up on the areas that interest you. Talk to people in the know. Visit a recruitment agency and get their insights. If you already know a secretary, take her out for a coffee and ask her about what she does, what she enjoys most about her work, and how she suggests you go about finding an area of interest within that arena.

Once you have decided what kind of secretary you want to be, you need to devise a plan to get to where you want to be. If, for instance, you decide that you want to be a secretary for a real estate developer because that is where your interest lies, your career plan will be different from that of someone who wants to be a medical secretary.

The wonderful thing about a secretarial career is that once you finish all the necessary training and are deemed a qualified professional, you are almost guaranteed success. In terms of training, the average secretary in the twenty-first century must have a combination of education and skills to qualify for even entry-level positions. Also referred to as junior secretaries, these entry-level roles will typically require the candidate to have at least a high school diploma, basic training in office administration and management, some computer knowledge, and a minimum of one to two years of experience. The more prominent the position, the more qualified and experienced the secretary must be. Secretaries who reach elite status do so because of a combination of higher education, an array of qualifications and many years of experience. When looking to fill the role of a senior executive secretary, some employers will require that the candidate have an undergraduate degree (or equivalent college diploma) and five to ten years of work experience. While some secretaries will rise through the ranks from lower-level clerical positions, they still require further education and training if they wish to reach the pinnacle of their field. If you are considering a secretarial career after high school, you must attend college and acquire the skills and training necessary to carry out the job. With the right attitude and qualifications, no junior secretary will ever remain junior forever. Progression is natural and should be expected.

Why else do people choose to be secretaries? Asking this question of those in the field will undoubtedly garner a range of answers: "My mother or my aunt was one," "genuine interest," "fell into it by accident," "financial considerations," "easiest route after high school," and so on.

Whatever your situation and motivation, you have to genuinely want to do the job in order to enjoy it and be good at it, otherwise you will be making the wrong decision.

The difficult part may be deciding on the area in which to work, but often you will determine this in the course of the job search. If you are applying through an employment agency, they will talk to you about areas that interest you and try to match your skills and interests with the right employer. Agencies can help to play a part in the decision-making process regarding the sector in which you end up working.

The Internet has simplified the job search process so that you can go to specific online job banks or sites to search for work according to whatever criteria you choose. For instance, you can narrow your search to specific industries, locations, titles, or compensation. If a search returns a favourable option, you can investigate further by visiting the prospective employer's own website and learning more about the company before submitting your application.

Job banks are useful. Not only do employers post their job openings directly on their websites, but the administrators of these job banks also post job advertisements that appear in local news publications, making it a one-stop shop. The job postings can encourage you to look at an industry you might not have considered in the past, and this can steer your career into a direction you never anticipated.

If you specifically choose to work in the government sector, be aware that certain departments will require security clearance before you can be hired. A criminal record check will be conducted, your background will be thoroughly investigated, and you will have to sign and adhere to a security code. Your conduct in public will also have to be above board, while you as a professional must remain mindful of your position at all times.

There are those who choose an industry that brings them the closest to what they might have chosen as a career had they been able to acquire the necessary qualifications. Dora, a paralegal, confided that she decided at the beginning of her secretarial training that she was going to work as a legal secretary and ultimately planned to stay within the legal field. Nine years later, when I asked her for the reasoning behind her decision, she replied,

> I never had the stamina or the funds to go to law school when I was growing up, even though at one stage I wanted to become a lawyer. I was quite keen on making money as soon as I possibly could. After working a few years as a junior legal secretary, I decided to take further training as a paralegal, which was less expensive, and the beauty of it was that I could study part time while working in the legal field. Ultimately, I reached my goal, but the best preparation I could have had for my current job was the stint I did as a junior legal secretary. I learned so much, and it was tremendous fun. I am happy now in my role as a paralegal because it encompasses legal secretarial work, so in a way my job hasn't changed. I am no longer pursuing the dream of becoming a lawyer even though I can finally afford to pay for my own education. I am just very content with what I am doing.

We live in a different world today, and better opportunities exist now than ever before—certainly more than what was available at the time Dora or I trained. Today you can dream big and achieve the seemingly impossible. If you happen to be interested in law and want to be a legal secretary, take a legal secretarial course, then join a law firm. You may start on the bottom rung as a junior legal secretary, but as long as you have a clear sense of where you are heading, you will not stay there for long. As a junior secretary, you get a rare and privileged front row seat from which to observe the professional lives of the higher echelon of whatever industry you choose. Use this opportunity to observe the work of legal secretaries, paralegals, lawyers and senior partners.

My reasons for becoming a secretary were complicated. After completing high school, I was very anxious to start working and earning my own money. Due to my circumstances, going out to work as soon as possible was the most sensible thing for me to do. I decided that my education would not stop; it would continue, but I would gain it on my own terms. I wanted to pay for my own education to ease the burden on my single mother. I was also very ambitious, and was resolute from the outset about taking as many of the courses as I could that would propel me to the top of my field. I decided that I wanted to be a secretary (among other things) and that I wanted to be one of the very best ones out there. For a little black girl living in sub-Saharan Africa to have such a clear vision and the tenacity to pronounce such bold aspirations was highly irregular for the time and place. While attending a select executive secretarial training program, I took on a part-time job as a telephonist/receptionist, and so my career began. Upon completion of the executive secretarial training program, I rose through the secretarial ranks very quickly. Just four years after commencing my career, I had been promoted thrice, and as a result I began working for high-powered executives at a very young age. This rapid rise to the top boosted my confidence and inspired me to travel to Europe so that I could acquire international working experience and further my education. At this early stage of my career, all my employers were very generous in allowing me to work and simultaneously continue my business education. At about the same time, one employer paid me the greatest compliment of my career. I was asked to organize the company's annual Worker of the Year awards event. Eager to do a good job, I threw myself into the role of event planner and was oblivious to all the other activities going on around me. It came as a complete surprise to me when the Worker of the Year award recipient turned out to be me. My career started out incredibly well and I have not looked back since, and the ride has been fulfilling and exhilarating.

I hope this personal example will reinforce the point I most want to make in this chapter: make a decision about where you want to go and what you want to do, and then go ahead and do it.

It is my belief that you need to be clear about your goals and where you are heading professionally. Not identifying your goals is detrimental to your future, since you cannot aim for something you don't know about. How can you tell when you have succeeded if you don't start out with a blueprint, goal, or vision? You need to chart your career and ensure that you will finish whatever you start. If you happen to start down the wrong path, you will soon find out. Almost always when such a dilemma arises, the universe also shows you a way out—an alternative career path.

If you are serious about becoming a secretary and choose to make secretarial work your lifelong vocation, then good for you. You are about to embark on a wonderfully fulfilling career with endless possibilities. Many of the secretaries that I know—and some whom I have interviewed for this book—are among the most privileged and contented professionals out there, and understandably so, because there is nothing better than landing the right job with the right boss.

Most of the secretaries I spoke to talked about how planning their careers and carefully selecting the industries that interested them the most contributed to their success. They felt that putting the time into reviewing their various areas of interest made the process easier and success that much sweeter, because they were succeeding in an area or industry where they wanted to be. For instance, one secretary might set out to work primarily in the investment sector for her entire career, while another might choose to work solely in the medical sector. It is entirely a matter of choice.

Twenty years ago when I entered the profession, the requirements were mainly good grammar, spelling, and letter composition, reasonably fast typing, good shorthand skills, and some formal education (at least a high school diploma). This was a tradition started in the 1920s, in an era when applicants for clerical jobs were expected to have a high school education.

Then, a kind of gold standard for the profession was set by the National Secretaries Association (NSA) via their first Certified Professional Secretaries Examination, which was first administered in 1951.[1] The

---

1 "About: History," *IAAP*, accessed November 5, 2010, http://www.iaap-hq.org/about/history.

association, based in Kansas City, Missouri (USA), was in 1998 renamed the International Association of Administrative Professionals (IAAP). There are representative IAAP chapters in most cities. A simple search on the Internet will reveal whether a chapter exists where you live, and if none exists you can look into the possibility of organizing one by contacting the organization.

Similarly in the UK and Ireland, Pitman Training is regarded as one of the most highly respected and recognized training organizations for secretaries. Initially developed for men by Sir Isaac Pitman,[2] the renowned inventor of shorthand, Pitman Training was established to provide training in office skills. Today there are hundreds of Pitman Training centres in Europe and around the world.

Computers brought about a shift in the minimum requirements to enter the field. Above and beyond the old standard requirements, secretaries had to retrain and/or acquire basic computer skills. In some cases, established and older secretaries who had entered the field thirty years prior, with nothing but their typing and stenographic skills, felt threatened by office automation. A few years into my secretarial career, I recall many conversations that I had with secretaries in positions senior to my own in which they painted a gloomy picture about my future. They expressed a great deal of anxiety and a strong belief that computers would at some point replace secretaries altogether. Given this angst, it is understandable that these veterans of the field did not embrace computers at the beginning. Now, in the twenty-first century, a secretary with no computer skills is unheard of. The role of secretary has changed drastically, and quite often the expectations can be unrealistic. Even the benchmark for a receptionist's position is not limited to the telephone and filing anymore, and computer skills are paramount.

A good secretary today is well educated, skilled in all aspects of her profession, adaptable to change, and aware that her position might encompass much more than the traditional secretarial job function.

2 "Isaac Pitman," *Answers.com*, accessed June 25, 2011, http://www.answers.com/topic/isaac-pitman.

Secretaries today are computer-savvy pseudo-managers who serve as the information clearinghouse for their departments or entire companies.

Summary

- Do your research first and amass a great deal of knowledge about secretarial work.
- Once you have made the decision, chart a course of where you want your career to take you and work towards that goal.
- Choose wisely. You may spend the better part of your life in this position, so you want to ensure that you enjoy what you are doing and, better still, look forward to going to work every morning.
- Ensure that you are comfortable with what the job calls for before submitting your application.
- Enhance your skills by taking all the right courses and update them regularly to give yourself an edge on the competition.
- Starting at the bottom can be a plus. Take in every experience, study those in higher positions than yours, and learn from their achievements and mistakes.
- Never lose sight of your goal and work towards it consistently.

Chapter 2: Secretarial Résumés

The structure and details of the résumé have evolved over time, but the basics remain the same. It is an honest snapshot of your education, skill set, and past employment. In some countries, especially in Europe, it is referred to as the curriculum vitae, or CV, which is derived from Latin – *curriculum* (course/program) *vitae* or *vitarum* (course of life). It is a brief account or point-form summary of your education, experience, and key achievements, particularly those applicable to the position for which you are applying.

When I took my secretarial training in the 1980s, a course on how to write one's own CV was part of the curriculum. That was some twenty years ago, and I have adjusted the content and layout of mine as the years progressed. I have gradually become enlightened about what it is employers look for in a CV or résumé.

Résumés are personal advertisements whose content and presentation convey a lot about their author. For secretaries, good presentation is important because it is part and parcel of the secretarial function. Grammar, spelling, punctuation, and basic letter design are considered to be a secretary's forte, and they are integral elements in clinching the initial interview.

The purpose of the résumé is not only to self-advertise but also to conjure up a certain curiosity that gives the reader an unconscious desire to want to meet you in person. If you market yourself well, the recruiter's interest will be piqued, and eventually he or she will want to meet you. The résumé itself will not get you the job, but it will get you a step closer to that all-important interview. It is at the interview that the employer or recruiter puts a face and a personality to the representation he or she has seen on paper.

During my career, I had occasion to work as a temporary employee (commonly referred to as a temp in secretarial circles) for a recruitment agency in Windsor, England. Some years later, while I was living in Calgary, Canada, I worked for an organization that afforded me the opportunity to learn about human resource administration and, more importantly, to participate in the recruitment process. Although these experiences were literally and figuratively oceans apart, the fundamentals were the same.

Working with the recruitment agency educated me about some key factors that most employers take into account when assessing the résumé.

- Upon receipt, the résumés were thoroughly screened for spelling, grammar, presentation, relevance, content, and competency.
- Recruiters had little patience for long, wordy documents and preferred aesthetically pleasing layouts, with short and concise bulleted paragraphs.
- Carelessly constructed documents were presumed to be a true reflection of the candidate's comportment.

Most recruitment agencies are guided by a mission statement, the driving force behind the way things are done. This is important because the recruitment agency business can be very competitive. Prospective and existing clients place a lot of trust in the agency's checks and balances, so such agencies simply cannot afford to look unprofessional. Their job is to deliver the best candidate to the client.

If you are taking a secretarial course that does not cover résumé writing, it would be prudent to request its inclusion. Course administrators may not have thought of it at the design stage and may welcome the suggestion. If not, they may suggest a book or a career centre that can assist you in preparing a professional résumé, particularly if it is your first. Many books have been written on how to prepare résumés. If time permits, spend half a day at your local library browsing through books on this topic, and you will come away a little more confident about preparing your own. If you can borrow one or two of these books from the library, do so, and then draft your résumé and have someone you trust review it, or visit a local career centre or recruitment agency and ask them to critique it for you. At the beginning of your career, these little steps are important to build your confidence about preparing your own résumé in the future.

Some entrepreneurial minds have made a business out of preparing professional résumés. Taking this route is entirely a matter of choice if you have the funds. Just remember that the résumé's purpose is to advertise you and your skills, so if someone else is writing it you need to take the time to sit down with the expert and let him or her explain what he or she has done with respect to content and layout. Also, be sure to provide some input into the preparation because the expert will not attend the interview with you. Your potential employer or recruiter will want *you* to describe the content of your résumé, and if something is included in it that you cannot speak to or substantiate, you not only diminish your chances of getting the job, you might come across as having embellished your credentials.

During the preparation stage of your résumé, determine what the prospective employer might be looking for. Read job advertisements carefully and compare the requirements with your own qualifications. They do not have to match one hundred percent. Remember that not all the qualifications the employer lists in the job description are "must-haves." Quite often they are, at least in part, an employer's wish list. Put yourself in the shoes of the person who will be reviewing your application. Keep that frame of mind until you have completed preparing the document, and this action will help ensure that your résumé is flawless.

In this modern age of computers and the Internet, many companies list employment opportunities on the "Careers" section of their websites, detailing a desired skill set. Quite often, a concise synopsis of the job requirements and desired skills to match are described on the webpage. It is important to read the requirements carefully. If the advertisement states that seventy words per minute (wpm) shorthand is a "must-have" and the best you can do is fifty-five words per minute, you will have to pass on the opportunity. Often, somewhere on the same page they will discourage those candidates who do not have matching skills from applying. In this instance, sending your résumé in even on speculation is a waste of time, as the employer has already been specific about "must-have" requirements.

Online Applications

Many companies are gravitating towards online applications, which require you to paste your cover letter and résumé into a specified section of a web page and submit your application online using this method only. If you want to apply for the job, you will have to do so using the preferred format. Be aware that there are certain guidelines by which online applications are reviewed favourably. These guidelines are generally not presented anywhere on the web page, and unless candidates have been taught how to complete online applications, it can be difficult to know what is acceptable and what is not.

Here are my tips for submitting online applications.

1. If you are required to paste your résumé and cover letter:
    - Keep your résumé clean, simple, short, and concise.
    - Use a simple font, such as Times New Roman 12 or Arial 12.
    - Font colour should always be black.
    - For continuity purposes, font and font size should be the same for both résumé and cover letter.
    - Do not leave large spaces between sections; compress your document as much as possible.
    - All text should be aligned to the left.

2. Be aware that many of these companies use customized point-driven recruitment software. In order to get a high score you need to make sure you spend time responding to each and

every question fully and honestly. In this case, whether you are shortlisted is determined by your score.

Some employers have gravitated towards this method to minimize the manpower involved in receiving and reviewing mounds of paper and the amount of filing involved. Furthermore, customized recruitment software programs help in the screening process by allocating a score for level of education, experience, and expertise. Naturally, the higher your score, the better your chances are to be shortlisted. All the information submitted online generally goes into a database where the employer can easily search for and review matching skills to job requirements for present and future positions. The plus side of this method for the candidate is that it saves time and money. You needn't worry too much about the layout of your résumé or the postage required for mailing your application. You submit it online in an instant. Environmentally conscious companies tend to favour this method. Access to a computer with Internet capability and an e-mail account is a *must*.

The Cover Letter

1. Use the same kind of paper for the letter as for the résumé; the two should not be different.
2. The letter should be addressed according to the instructions provided on the vacancy notice or advertisement. If there was no specific individual noted as the person to write to, address the letter to the "Recruiting Manager" if responding to an employment agency and to the "Hiring Manager" when writing directly to the company. Cite the position you are applying for, and then quote any applicable job reference numbers in the subject line.
3. If there is an individual you have to address the letter to, then for goodness' sake, spell his or her name correctly! Similarly, the company name and address to which you are applying should not be misspelled. If you are uncertain, call the receptionist at the company to which you are applying and double-check these important facts rather than guessing.

4. Format the letter exactly as the résumé, using the same professional fonts and font sizes. Given the length of the résumé in comparison to the letter, the font size may be slightly different, but the difference should be minimal. Margins should be 1–1.25 inches wide at the sides and 1 inch at the top and bottom.
5. Aim to make the cover letter nothing more than a simple introduction about you, the candidate. What you say here reflects your level of experience and intellect.
6. Respond specifically to the job requirements, emphasizing how your qualifications and experience make you the ideal candidate for the position.
7. Succinctly capture the essence of who you are in the cover letter and endeavour to sell yourself as a smart team player who will add great value to the organization involved. Your goal in the cover letter should be to entice the recruiter to want to read more about you and, better still, meet you in person.
8. Keep your paragraphs short and to the point; the cover letter itself should be no more than one page.
9. Although the cover page is important and ideally must accompany a résumé, bear in mind that the recruiter will give your letter a very quick read and then move on to the résumé, which is where his or her interest really lies.

Check, double-check, and triple-check the grammar and spelling, and have someone else do it for you as well.

Figure 1 - Cover Letter Template

{Insert Your Address Line 1}
{Insert Your Address Line 2}
{Insert Date}
The Hiring Manager
{Insert Company Name}
{Insert Address Line 1}
{Insert Address Line 2}
Dear *Hiring Manager*,
RE: *{Insert position being applied for and reference number}*
Paragraph 1:
Declare your interest in the position. Tell the recruiter how you became aware of the position and why you chose to pursue the opportunity.
Paragraph 2:
Talk about the skills and strengths you bring to the position, giving brief and precise examples of your most recent accomplishments. Review the duties and responsibilities stated in the advertisement and highlight your experience in those areas. For example, if experience preparing packages for board meetings is required, you should highlight any such experience in your cover letter.
Paragraph 3:
Make a strong closing statement that not only persuades the recruiter to read your résumé but also leaves him or her with the impression that he or she would be remiss in not pursuing you as a potential candidate.
Closing:
Sincerely,
{Insert your name}
Enclosure

Checklist for Résumé Preparation

1. Decide on a format and stick to it. The most common formats for secretarial are the chronological résumé, which lists work experience from earliest to most recent, and reverse chronological (preferred by most employers and more commonly used in this arena), which starts off with the most recent or current position and moves backwards to your first employer.
2. Remember, your résumé should be no more than two pages, with your cover letter being the first. Stay away from fancy fonts. They may look impressive to you, but the recruiter is only interested in your qualifications and education, not your design prowess. It also doesn't look professional, as it implies that you have spent more time playing with the font than you have writing the content.
3. Keep the font simple. Good fonts are Arial, Times New Roman, Tahoma, CG Times, Century Gothic, Garamond, and Courier New.
4. Keep the paper white or as close to white as possible. Although some self-help books may encourage off-white, my advice is that you should find high-quality, non-glossy true white paper and purchase a ream of it to ensure that you do not run out and end up using different shades of white for each page. Many intend to have their résumé stand out by using fancy, colourful paper, but the effect on the recruiter or employer will definitely be opposite to the desired reaction! Remember, a résumé is a professional document that is likely to be photocopied and shared with a number of people who have an interest in the position you are applying for. This document sharing could be via photocopying and then hand distribution, or facsimile transmission. As such, the quality of your paper is important.
5. The very top of each page should show your full name, home address, e-mail address, and contact telephone numbers.

6. The recruiter or employer never intends to read your application as if it were a novel about your life. He or she receives thousands of submissions for any given job posting and has little time to read a long, wordy document loaded with irrelevant information. Whoever is reviewing your submission merely gives your document an ocular scan, noting what's relevant to the vacant position. Therefore, use short but concise paragraphs, preferably in point form. Should the recruiter require elaboration on any point, he or she will have to make arrangements to ask you in person, won't they?
7. Try to tailor your résumé to the position. That is, if the position requires some accounting background, include all accounting-related work that you have done in the past, highlighting your key achievements and strengths in that particular area.
8. Your résumé should be specific about the roles you have had in the past, the skills you developed in those roles, and all relevant major accomplishments. Certain skill sets could prove to be a feather in your cap, since many secretarial functions are ultimately interrelated, and the more knowledge you have, the better off you are. For instance, while experience in a legal department may not necessarily be directly pertinent when applying to work for a chief financial officer or a chief hospital administrator, the depth of your knowledge and education may still impress an employer and give you an edge over another candidate.
9. Do not embellish the facts to impress. It won't work, and you are likely to get caught. Recruiters and employers do check and cross-reference all the information you provide, and any educational claims you make will be verified. I personally carried out this task in the past. Bear in mind that you could be challenged in an interview about the claims on your résumé; you could be asked to elaborate on your education, where you studied, for how long, et cetera. Any fabrications or exaggerations will be easy to pick up on in an interview setting and will undermine your credibility.

10. Highlight titles of positions using bold, underlining, or a slightly larger font size than the body text.
11. Duties entailed should be listed functionally and in summary form. Bulleted lists are easier to read.
12. When recruiters visually scan your résumé, they are generally looking for the buzzwords pertinent to the position that were used in the job posting, so be sure to include them in your résumé. These buzzwords refer to specific and related experience transferable to the position at hand. For instance, for a secretarial position, the buzzwords could include "shorthand experience," "Dictaphone experience," "proofreading," "scheduling meetings," "making travel arrangements," event coordination," "multitasking," "self-starter personality," "project management experience," and so on.
13. Tenure is important, and therefore all dates should be highlighted in bold type. Many employers are interested in finding out how long you held a particular position in order to establish whether you remain at one job for a reasonable length of time, which speaks about your sense of commitment. Early on in my career, a recruiter pointed out that I appeared to move from one job to another every two years, an observation that she felt warranted an explanation. At that point, I had none. Although her observation was true, this was news to me and provided a good learning opportunity.
14. I cannot emphasize this enough: check, double-check, and triple-check for correct punctuation, spelling, and grammar. Spelling errors in particular are unacceptable, as they show a lack of attention to detail.
15. Whether preparing a résumé or curriculum vitae, be sure to always include your full name, home address, e-mail address, and contact telephone numbers. Also, be aware that when applying for jobs in other countries using online job applications, you may be asked to state in your resume or cover letter that you have permission to work in that particular country.

16. When sending an application via regular mail, I prefer to send all three pages loose and unstapled. However, this is debatable and a matter of choice. Some recruiters prefer that you staple all three pages together, as they receive hundreds of résumés and it is quite possible for them to misplace loose pages.
17. Once your résumé is ready to go via mail, please do not fold the documents. Instead, use a full-size A4 envelope. If at all possible, do not handwrite the address on the envelope. A printed label looks much more professional. However, if it can't be helped do not worry too much about the envelope; by the time the document reaches the hands of the recruiter, it will have been discarded. Generally, a receptionist or clerk will have opened your envelope and stamped the contents with the date and time of receipt.
18. Finally, before posting your envelope, have it weighed and be sure you have the correct postage!

The E-résumé

In my years of working at the senior management level, I observed countless times how a résumé can pass from hand to hand within an organization. In this day and age of e-mail correspondence, your résumé could almost be called an e-résumé, if submitted via e-mail. When you submit your application or résumé to someone for consideration via electronic mail (e-mail), he or she may forward it on to another interested party, who might forward it to someone else, and so on. It is a fact that most companies now only accept job applications electronically, either via e-mail or a section on their website, where you are required to "upload" your résumé. Rarely do people send résumés via regular mail in these fast times we live in. When you are submitting your e-résumé for consideration, try to stick to widely accepted formats for attached documents, such as Microsoft Word or PDF. (From Word 2007 onward, it is possible to save any Word doc as a PDF.) Do remember that whatever software version you have used to type your document may not be the same at the destination computer. Other applications may be rejected by the host computer if the format is unfamiliar or if they cannot be scanned for viruses. When in doubt, call the employer to verify that they received your résumé – it's a wise decision, and there is nothing wrong with doing so. If you are slightly dubious about submitting your application via e-mail, you should contact the employer and request permission to make your submission via fax instead. Even fax machines are not all that reliable, though. If you do submit your application via facsimile, you must call to verify that the document was received. The fax machine at the other end could be out of paper, non-responsive, or malfunctioning, or you may have faxed to the wrong number. All are reasonable possibilities that must be considered.

Figure 2 - Résumé Template

{Insert Your Full Name}

{Insert Your Personal Data: Address, Telephone Number and E-Mail}

Professional Summary

Encapsulate the career highlights that set you apart from other candidates. This is an opportunity to sell yourself and encourage the recruiter to read the rest of your résumé.

What strengths do you bring to the position?

What accomplishments are you most proud of?

Why are you the best candidate for the job?

Work Experience

Provide information about your employment history in chronological order, beginning with your most recent or current employer.

{Insert company name and City}

{Insert the dates of your employment}

{Insert your job title}

List the duties and/or responsibilities of the job

Education & Professional Development

{Education &Professional Development can also be placed before or after the work experience}

Provide information about your education in chronological order, starting with the most recent achievements.

Date	**Accomplishment**	**Institution**
Year	Degree, Diploma or Certificate	University/College/School name

Computer Experience

Computer skills are of paramount importance in the secretarial occupation. Your competence in all the major software programs deserves to be highlighted in the résumé.

Software Program	**Proficiency Level**
{Example: Microsoft Word	*Insert your level of experience,*

example: Expert*}*

Memberships, Awards, and Hobbies

This area is sometimes labelled as "Other." Here you can provide information about professional and volunteer organizations that you belong to, including any awards you have received.

References

If you choose to, you can provide at least three references who are not members of your family, preferably previous managers that you reported to directly. Alternatively, you can simply state that your *references are available upon request.*

Summary

- Let your cover letter entice the recruiter to read your résumé.
- When addressing your letter of application directly to a specific person as quoted in the vacancy announcement or posting, ensure you spell his or her name correctly!
- Include the full company address in the cover letter. If it is not posted in the vacancy announcement, seek out the full address by contacting the receptionist at the company, visiting the company's website on the Internet or checking the most recent edition of the white or yellow pages.
- Use a spellchecker on your cover letter as well as your résumé.
- Peruse both documents for grammatical errors and correct them.
- A haphazardly written résumé will read the same way it is written: without much thought, indicating that it was quickly thrown together with little consideration for the chronological flow, formatting, or grammar.
- Remember the résumé represents *you*, so ensure that it justly captures all you have to offer to a prospective employer.

- Get someone whose opinion you value to critique it for you.
- First impressions are everything. Does your résumé impress you? Does it stand out? Switch places with the recruiter and critique it yourself.
- **Do not** embellish facts about your education, qualifications, or work history. You will get caught!
- Your résumé must be honest, concise, and professionally written.
- Follow the submission guidelines as stipulated by the employer.
- Recruiters are notoriously hard-nosed about résumé and interview etiquette; you only get one shot – if you snooze, you lose.
- Although most employers may promise to keep your résumé on file should you not be successful in obtaining a position, it will be very difficult to remain at the top of a recruiter's mind for other opportunities if your résumé does not pass any of the gatekeepers mentioned above. Irrespective of what the recruiter thinks of your résumé at the time of receipt, I encourage job seekers to follow up with a phone call or an e-mail enquiring on the status of your application or other job openings at the firm. Bear in mind that recruiters often receive hundreds of résumés, and an e-mail might stir them to review your résumé and possibly invite you in for an initial, informal interview. Recruiters love enthusiastic candidates.

Chapter 3: Interview Guidelines

Interviews are a reality of the job search process. They have to be done, and there is no getting around them. When you are in the market for a new job, being asked to attend an interview is a very good thing because it tells you that the employer is impressed or intrigued by your application. Getting an interview means that you have your foot in the door of that organization and could well be a strong contender for the job. Awareness of what to expect and advance preparation will enhance your confidence during the interview and greatly increase your chances of getting the position.

Each interview session is different from the next because of the complex dynamics involved. There needs to be the right chemistry between the interviewer(s) and the interviewee. Generally and ideally, there will be more than one person conducting the interview. This helps to deflect accusations of bias, discrimination, unfairness, and prejudice. A panel will usually consist of the hiring manager (who will most likely be your future boss) and a representative from the company's human resources department.

I can remember every single interview that I have ever attended – bizarre but true. The reason they are so vivid in my memory is that I learned something new at each one about both the process and myself. I also know why I lost some of the jobs I applied for – but hindsight is 20/20. Judging from my previous experience, I came to realize that the outcome of an interview for a secretary is influenced by her ability to score top marks for the following prerequisites:

- Presentation
- Non-verbal communication or cues
- Confidence and verbal communication skills

- Knowledge and expertise
- Experience
- Good fit
- Motivation
- Availability
- Interview preparedness

Presentation

For secretarial positions, your presentation at the interview is extremely important. First impressions count for everything and can increase or ruin your chances of getting the job. An interviewer's impression is formed in the first few seconds after you walk into the room, and remarkably, those few seconds are what you will be remembered by. If you enter and the prospective employer is appalled at or unimpressed by your overall presentation, you will have to work extremely hard in the interview to win him over. Anything could put the interviewer off, be it your choice of attire, hairstyle, demeanour, or even your smile (or lack thereof). The list is endless. Body language can make a difference to your total image, sometimes a big one. You might say such judgements are not fair, but it is an employer's prerogative. Employers know the calibre of personnel they would like on their staff and the type of person whom they don't want.

The same first impression principles that apply to a blind date or the chemistry that can occur between people when they meet for the first time can be likened to the interview encounter. Why do some people click instantly, while others do not? It starts with that all-important first impression and progresses to various other factors, such as non-verbal cues and communication. If you are, at a minimum, well presented, approachable, confident, eloquent, friendly, and engaging, you will attain the desired reaction. Your goal is to present a balanced and true image of yourself – not over-the-top and false, yet not bland either. The overall presentation should never detract from the message you want to convey, so ensure that your clothes or hairstyle do not speak so loudly that your intended audience cannot hear what *you* are saying!

When applying for a secretarial position at a prominent level (which generally means working for a senior executive such as a president, CEO, general manager, or senior vice president), your overall presentation should exude poise, confidence, professionalism, and a polished demeanour. Dress should be appropriate for the interview, preferably tailored business attire. (See figure 3 for guidelines.)

Figure 3 - Interview Dress Guide for Women

ITEM	APPROPRIATE	INAPPROPRIATE
SUIT:	• Tailored classic business suit, preferably in navy, gray, or black hues, in suitable fabric weight for the season • Smooth, clean lines and surfaces with no pattern are best • Fitted to semi-fitted classic tailored jacket – paired with: • a tailored skirt – straight classic cut pencil or contoured knee length, A-line or midi, or • tailored dress pants – simple, classic, plain front, must match the jacket, or • a dress (dress suit) – sleeveless or short-sleeved sheath or shift	• Awfully tight clothing, particularly skirt, pant, or dress • Extremely dated or overly trendy suit • Miniskirt/dress • Very bright colours such as red, yellow, and green, or fabrics with too much sheen • Thigh-high slits, tight-fitting, frilly, asymmetrical, or overly trendy style skirt/dress

SEPARATES:	• If you do not own a suit, combine matching or coordinated separates in order to closely resemble a suit: • Tailored sport jacket or blazer • Clean cut tailored dress pants • Plain tailored skirt with clean lines • Tailored shift/sheath dress worn with coordinated blazer or jacket	• Leather jacket, sweater, or cardigan • Cocktail dress or attire more suited for evening social events • Denim • Garments with visible brand/logo monograms • Heavy, gaudy, shiny, or heavily patterned fabrics • Off-the-shoulder, strapless, or sun dress • Shorts, Bermuda pants, Capri pants • Uncoordinated and competing patterns
SHIRT **OR** **BLOUSE:**	• Shirt with collar that coordinates well with your suit, or • Nice understated blouse in neutral colours that coordinates well with your suit • Try monotone colours that match your suit, such as a shade of blue, gray, or black, to create an interesting contrast	• Any top that displays racist or similarly offensive messages, words, terms, slogans, pictures, or cartoons • Glitzy evening style top with excessive glitter or sequins • Indecent, low cut, suggestive top or blouse • T-shirt of any kind • Top or blouse with garish animal or floral prints
HOSIERY:	• Sheer pantyhose or trouser socks (natural, muted black or navy, ideally should match trouser/skirt hue)	• Fishnet or patterned tights or stockings

ACCESSORIES:		
COAT/HAT:	• Coat: classic and formal in conservative colours (black, blue, or camel) • Hat: appropriate if worn outside and removed once indoors. • Exception: when head gear is worn for religious or health related purposes	• Wearing a hat, head band, or any head gear for fashionable purposes indoors.
SHOES:	• Closed-toe and heel, leather or suede, court or classic pumps, 2- or 3-inch heel is ideal. 4-inch heel is maximum; ideally should match your outfit (black is always safe)	• Any open-toed shoe (sandals, very high heeled stilettos [more than 4 in], tennis / running shoes, flip-flops, peep-toes
HANDBAG:	• Professional small to medium-sized tote or handbag (black or dark brown) • Leather briefcase/ attaché case for your documents (black or dark brown)	• Evening, designer, or oversized handbag
JEWELLERY:	• Small to medium-sized gold, silver, or pearl studs, or unobtrusive drop earrings • Engagement ring and wedding band if married • Wristwatch	• Any more than one ring per hand • Chunky, gaudy bracelets and neck chains • Facial jewellery: nose and eyebrow rings
GLASSES:	• Simple and professional clear reading glasses that complement your face shape	• Oversized or gaudy tinted spectacles or sunglasses

GROOMING:	• Always practice good grooming and personal hygiene • For interviews your hair should be professionally cut to frame your face in a simple style, or tied back into a chignon • Makeup: a minimal and natural look is appropriate • Fragrance should either be avoided or be extremely light and subtle • Never leave home without checking yourself in the mirror (full length and back to front)!	• Heavily plied makeup • Heavy, lingering scents, or perfume and cologne • Bouffant or outrageous hairstyle

If you are uncertain about what to wear, engage the services of a certified and reputable image consultant and you are unlikely to go wrong, especially if this is a position you absolutely must get. You cannot afford any mishaps, even in the clothes department. Should you also be lucky enough to be the successful candidate, it would be prudent to continue working with an image consultant in order to keep your look current and appropriate. Image consultants can be found in most major cities by searching the Internet, the yellow pages, or through word of mouth.

Some employers are quite pedantic about carrying forward the rules of yesteryear into the twenty-first century. For instance, women attending interviews in business pantsuits may be unacceptable in one establishment and yet acceptable in another. In some of today's young, avant-garde, and so-called hip offices, this issue is immaterial, and whether you come dressed traditionally in a skirted suit or otherwise will likely go completely unnoticed. If you are comfortable and confident wearing a pantsuit to an interview, then proceed to do so. Be aware, however, that if your interviewer is old fashioned, you might lose marks for that alone. Nowadays, some people view traditional interview guidelines as outdated. In my opinion, the whole debate over dress/skirt suit versus pantsuit issue needs to be revised for modern times. Modern tailored pantsuits for women look very professional and business appropriate. In fact, the tailored pantsuit is my business attire of choice. It is very important, though, that there be absolutely no décolletage; it is as inappropriate in an interview setting as it is in any business environment.

I would caution interviewees on the issue of dressing provocatively at interviews, as this might lead to certain unflattering presumptions being made about you and could cost you a wonderful opportunity. Any slits on skirts or dresses should be conservative and relegated to the posterior. Avoid thigh-high slits – these are tacky and unsuitable at an interview. (See figure 3 for guidelines.)

I once applied for a senior secretarial position in the heart of rural Kent, England. When I called for directions to get to the interview, I was told to expect a very casual environment. I took this as a hint to make sure my attire would suit the workplace and wore a business casual outfit consisting of a tailored shirt and blazer paired with untailored casual pants. The term business casual simply means dressing less formally while still being suitably attired to conduct business. Once again, the expertise of an image consultant can be useful in such a situation because he or she can assist you in achieving the right image for any given scenario. Engaging the services of an image consultant can take away the anxiety of deciding what to wear to a non-conventional interview setting.

A rural environment is governed by different dress rules than those of a major city, so careful thought is required. If you are uncertain or cannot afford to engage the services of an image consultant, stick to the tailored business suit and you will not go wrong, because a suit is generally expected and accepted. Presentation is only one small determining factor in securing the job but is essential because it is part and parcel of that all-important first impression. Experience, knowledge, expertise, and enthusiasm are also considered in the final analysis.

No matter what you wear to an interview, you must learn to pay attention to the details. A missing button on your shirt could cost you a job opportunity. It may sound trivial, but it communicates to the employer that you are possibly haphazard and that once employed, you will pay little attention to the small details. It could convey the impression that you are careless about your image and may, in turn, care little about the quality of your output at work.

Years back, I sat on an interviewing panel where a young woman came to be interviewed for a junior secretarial position. The interview itself went quite well for the candidate, and at one stage it seemed as if she might be a contender for the shortlist. However, at the end of the interview, as she stood up and bid us good-bye, she turned to leave the room, and in full view of the panel was a very inappropriate thigh-high slit and unravelling hemline. The stitching had come apart from the seam and was hanging unattractively from the back of her skirt, with little bits of loose thread visible. There was horror on the face of each panellist, and even though her attire was never discussed she wasn't placed on the short list of potential candidates. We primarily focused on discussing her performance during the interview and scored according to her responses to the interview questions. However, in the final analysis, her appearance as she exited the room seemed to colour each panellist's decision not to call her back. I later discovered that her appearance and presentation marks had dragged her overall score down.

Appearance and presentation do matter because they not only convey your self-respect and personal integrity but also communicate, however subtly, how you will conduct yourself in a business environment.

Dress rules for men are simpler in comparison to those for women. The old-fashioned rule is to dress in a suit in the generally accepted darker, muted tones of navy blue, black, or gray, paired with a clean white or light blue shirt. For some unknown reason, men in brown suits conjure up distrust. The hue itself is simply not suitable for interviews and should be avoided. Pinstriped suits in black, gray, or navy are most common. Some men can get away with wearing separates and mixing two colours, such as black and blue or black and gray, in the form of a different-coloured jacket and pant. If the attire looks professional, some interviewers will note the mismatch but choose to ignore it on account of the candidate's strength in the other categories. The shirt should be clean and coordinate well with the suit. The tie should be understated. Avoid bright bold prints and patterns, and steer clear of bright colours in the red and yellow family, because the focus will become your garish tie as opposed to your face.

(See figure 4 for guidelines.)

Figure 4 - Interview Dress Guide for Men

ITEM	APPROPRIATE	INAPPROPRIATE
SUITS AND JACKETS	• Tailored, classic-style business suit, preferably single breasted • Medium to lightweight fabrics in 100% wool/wool blend • Conservative colours: muted darker shade such as black, charcoal, gray, or navy • Pinstriped suits should have solid, pencil-thin stripes	• Designer or flamboyant silk suit • Tight and ill-fitting suit • Wide or thick horizontal, diagonal, curved, or wavy lines in suits

SEPARATES:	• If you do not own a suit, combine matching or coordinated separates in order to closely resemble a suit. • Tailored sport jacket or blazer • Clean cut tailored trousers, wrinkle resistant with plain front; basic one-inch cuff or uncuffed; appropriate length is slightly over ankle and dusting mid-part of dress shoe	• Any type of leather jacket • Uncoordinated and competing patterns • Cardigan or sweater • Casual and untailored attire • Denim, khaki, or Dockers pants • Garments with visible brand/ logo monograms • Shorts, baggy pants, sweat pants
SHIRTS AND TIES:	• Shirt: 100% woven broadcloth or cotton blend with long sleeves and a straight collar; white or off-white and spotless; stripes should be pencil thin; aim for a clean and simple effect • Tie: if you can afford it, get one that is 100% silk, and if not, seek out a sales associate at a menswear store for assistance in acquiring an affordable and appropriate tie suitable for an interview; it should be understated with either a simple pattern or no pattern with strong dark-light contrast to jacket and shirt	• Plaid and any bright collared shirt • Gaudy tie in bold patterned prints • Turtleneck sweater, golf or polo shirt • T-shirt of any kind or colour • Unbuttoned shirt

ACCESSORIES:		
COAT AND HAT:	• Knee-length cashmere or wool blend, or a trench coat. Hues: black, navy blue or camel • Bowler/Fedora worn outside (going to the interview) but must be removed once inside. • Exception: when head gear is worn for religious or health related purposes	• Wearing a hat or headband in the interview • Coat with animal print or fur
SHOES AND SOCKS:	• Leather lace-ups in black or brown, depending on suit colour • The rule for socks is to closely match the hue of your trousers	• Moccasins, sandals, flip-flops, decorative shoes or sneakers • White or other brightly collared socks
BRIEFCASE:	• Black or brown leather/faux leather, preferably underarm portfolio case	• Using a paper or plastic bag to carry your papers!
GLASSES:	• Simple and clear reading glasses appropriately styled that complement your facial shape	• Oversized or tinted spectacles or sunglasses
JEWELLERY:	• Wristwatch and/or wedding band	• Facial jewellery, gold chains and bracelets, gaudy and excessive numbers of rings
GROOMING:	• Practice good grooming and personal hygiene • Hair should be professionally cut to frame your face • Use minimal aftershave and cologne • Check in the mirror (full length and back to front) before heading out the door!	• Poor grooming: body door, heavy cologne or aftershave, unkempt beard or moustache

For men, polished shoes communicate a lot about the wearer. Even if you are a male candidate who happens to be attending his very first interview with little experience or the financial wherewithal to afford a professional shoeshine, do make an effort to clean your shoes. Ensuring that they are presentable will garner you points on presentation and impress a prospective employer. I can recall another situation where I was part of the interviewing panel and we were evaluating the candidates after a long interviewing session. A member of the panel announced that she was granting top marks to the candidate with the crisp, clean shirt and polished shoes because she was so impressed with his effort to look presentable – more evidence proving that recruiters observe every single thing during the interview. Never be deluded into thinking that they do not notice the minor details. Even those considered to be very good communicators with expert knowledge about the position being offered must rise to the occasion and be aware that appearance is one of the major contributors to the final decision. Attending an interview in too-casual attire is not recommended, particularly for office work. Jeans are not suitable for interviews for secretarial positions unless this is stipulated as acceptable prior to the interview.

A colleague once told me about a male secretary who had an ideal job working as a writer's assistant in Banff, Alberta, Canada, and went to work dressed in jeans every day. This is an obvious exception to the rule, but unless this male secretary was told to attend the interview in casual clothes, he would have had to adhere to the same principles reinforced in this chapter and go in tailored business attire in order to present a professional image and show respect for the interviewers.

A previous employer of mine in London, England, whose chief function was to carry out interviews for accounting professionals helped illuminate the behind-the-scenes process for screening candidates to me. While working at this establishment, part of my job was to pull the candidates' files prior to their arrival for an interview, review the notes, and ensure that all the information on their paper files was fully updated in the computer system. Some of the comments about the candidates were quite brutal, and what surprised me the most was the fact that the recruiting consultants picked up on every minute detail. Comments such as: "Personal appearance less than professional," "Overbearing cheap perfume," "Inappropriate attire," and "Poor grooming" were commonplace. Equally common were comments on confidence, delivery, poise, and overall presentation. It was here that I learned firsthand some of the dos and don'ts of interviews that have stood me in good stead whenever I have attended them.

Non-verbal Communication

We are all guilty of observing people and trying to "read" them without talking to them. What we are trying to read are their non-verbal cues, or body language. Everything about our body language is powerful and can even be more potent in its message than verbal communication. In an interview setting, people form impressions based on non-verbal cues, including the way you carry yourself, the way you shake someone's hand, your smile, your gestures, and what you do with your hands. Sitting in an interview with a CEO whom I was hoping to impress into hiring me as his assistant, I thought I had my emotions and cues in check until, towards the end of the interview, he asked, "Are you less nervous now?" I was surprised by the comment and asked him if I had looked nervous at any point in the interview. He replied in the affirmative. Unbeknownst to me, I had been sitting on the edge of my chair with my hands clasped in a way that he interpreted as nervousness. By my own calculation, I really wasn't nervous at all but rather was listening very intently and was a little too eager to please. Nonetheless, it mattered little what I thought. His interpretation was his own, and I couldn't change that. I wasn't hired. You might argue that interviewers should never judge a book by its cover, but judge they will, whether you like it or not. It is human nature. Recruiting managers are in the business of human relations, and they watch for and understand how to interpret non-verbal communication. What you intend and what they interpret can be completely different. When invited to attend an interview, it is important to be self-aware and attempt to control your body language as much as is feasibly possible in order to ensure that your non-verbal cues are in sync with the message you want to convey. Nearly everyone who attends an interview wants to appear confident, poised, smart and in control. The following non-verbal cues could help you garner that favourable first impression.

- Walk tall, purposefully, and with lots of energy.
- You do not have to do anything to prove you are a good person or that you are better than anyone else; just be yourself, and your overall presentation, behaviour, and mannerisms will convey the true sense of who you are.
- Your facial expression should communicate openness, interest, and an air of self-assurance.
- Plant a genuine smile on your face when appropriate.
- Do not be defensive and on guard. Be genuine, open, and receptive.
- Overall posture should be erect and exude confidence – not cockiness, but simply the confidence of someone who is comfortable in her own skin.
- Your handshake should be firm, and palms should be devoid of sweat or grease.
- Wait to be told where to sit, and do so slowly and elegantly.
- When invited to sit in an open forum, sit erect and do not slouch, and minimize the crossing and uncrossing of legs.
- When invited to sit at a large boardroom table where your legs are not visible, there is no need to worry about your leg movements – just do what is comfortable.
- Minimize hand gestures. Use gestures that come to you naturally and are not forced, because this will come through.
- Do not clasp, steeple, or wring your hands, and never, ever fold your arms across your chest at an interview.
- Keep your hands away from your face or hair (this is hard to do, but it communicates nervousness or slight reticence).
- Maintain eye contact with whoever is speaking to you.
- Male candidates should avoid adjusting their ties during an interview. This action can be misconstrued as vain, shifty, or downright arrogant.

Confidence and Verbal Communication Skills

Once your overall presentation has been assessed, it's down to business. The interviewers want to hear you speak, so they will direct well-crafted questions at you and then carefully note your responses. Confidence and verbal communication skills go hand in hand; you cannot have one without the other. Your communication skills will be that much better and even more impressive if you are confident, and vice versa. Your voice is another window to your soul. A great deal about the characteristics of a person can be gleaned from the tone and inflection in her voice alone. The tone of your voice should match the intent of your message, or the meaning will be lost. Inflection refers to alterations in the pitch and tone of your voice. Adjust the volume of your voice to match the mood, but be aware that maintaining the same tone with no inflection can make you sound monotonous. Speaking too slowly or too rapidly also makes listening difficult. If you attend the interview genuinely interested in learning about the company and are enthused about the job opportunity, chances are you will respond very naturally to the interviewing process. Generally, when a candidate has the relevant experience or education behind them, confidence comes naturally.

When you attend an interview for the very first time the process can be quite nerve-racking, which is understandable. However, recruiters are very astute, and if they know that it is your very first interview, they will disregard your nervous responses. What recruiters and/or employers look for in first-time candidates is genuine enthusiasm, eagerness, an honest self-representation on the part of the candidate, and her suitability to the role. An employer may forgive lack of confidence if these prerequisites are met.

Talking to recruiters and bosses about the interview process, I gleaned some key requirements for someone to be considered a contender for a position. Recruiters and bosses dislike candidates who "put on an act" during an interview. One recruiter labelled them as "flakes." The first thing a boss looks for in his potential secretary is authenticity. Be authentic and be yourself. An executive pointed out to me that when he's in the process of hiring a secretary, it is important to him that she engages in a dialogue and doesn't respond to interview questions with one-word answers. "Getting a blank stare is a complete turn-off for me," he told me. Perhaps author Gerard Egan put it best when he succinctly described effective dialogue as "Turn-taking … I speak. You speak."[3] The salient point is that an interview is a two-way street, where the interviewee must connect with the interviewer(s). A dialogue, not a monologue, must take place. Contrary to popular belief, a secretary can influence the outcome of an interview. I interviewed a senior executive who was dismayed at candidates who find it difficult to come up with a single question at an interview. "It is astounding! How can you *not* have any questions about a position for which you are applying or an organization you want to join?" he asked irritably.

A helpful confidence-builder is practice. Practice what you are going to say by listing on a piece of paper all your past achievements, goals, and work methodology. If you have some experience attending interviews, you will have a fair idea of the type of questions you will be asked. Ask a friend to practice with you by having him or her interview you, and this exercise will go a long way towards boosting your confidence.

Knowledge and Expertise

As soon as you are invited to attend an interview, you must research the company and familiarize yourself with its history, management team, mission statement, overall vision, and number of employees. Ideally, as a candidate you will be familiar with the industry to which you are applying, but if not, the comprehensive research that you do in preparation for the interview will give you the solid foundation you need to fully appreciate and evaluate your suitability for the role you are being asked to play. A good place to start your research is the Internet. Visit the prospective employer's website and conduct a thorough review of the company's mandate. Follow this up with a review of your own skills,

3 Gerard Egan, with assistance from Richard F. McGourty and Hany Shamshoum, *Skilled Helping Around the World* (Belmont, CA: Thomson Brooks/Cole, 2005).

experience, and career goals, seeing how they fit in with the overall culture and corporate vision. On a piece of paper ask and answer the following questions:

- What do I know about this company?
- Can I make a difference at this organization, and if so, how?
- Why should this company hire me, and what do I bring to the table?

This exercise will further boost your confidence and assist in your preparation. During the interview, you may be asked "behavioural-type" questions that explore past situations and will show how you demonstrated the required skills to handle those situations. These types of questions are based on what is commonly known in HR circles as the STAR (situation/task, action, and result) interview technique. Using the STAR system, the interviewer may give you a scenario and then ask you to describe a similar positive or negative work situation and how you applied yourself to affect the outcome. (See figure 6 for sample STAR questions.)

Listen closely to the questions and respond very carefully. Do not make things up to give yourself an edge or to appear as an expert in areas you know nothing about. If you cannot come up with a quick and specific answer to the question, say, "I do not recall such an experience in my career, however ..." and offer a suggestion about how you could handle such a situation if it occurred. Avoid rambling on needlessly or over-answering questions. Just be honest and to the point. If you are not sure about a question, ask that it be repeated or for an example. Remember that your interviewers simply want to know if you can do the job at hand. Highlight your strengths eloquently and your weaknesses honestly but carefully.

For instance, if the interviewer asks you, "What do you consider to be your greatest weakness?" – which of course, as you know, is a trick question, and the "trick" answer must be one that turns a negative into a positive – the best way to deal with this question is to be ready for it. When it is asked of you, don't spend an eternity in front of the recruiter trying to conjure up the perfect, on-the-spot answer that you think they want to hear. You need to consider this question in your interview preparation and be ready to answer it honestly. In order to turn a negative into a positive, you might say, "My biggest weakness is learning to deal with the downtimes in the course of the day." Quickly turn this negative into a positive by continuing on to state that you are someone who likes to stay busy and that you have learned to motivate yourself by finding new projects where you can be of assistance.

Another response you can use might be, "Being a bit of perfectionist is a big weakness of mine." You can turn this negative into a positive by continuing to state that you always want to do the best job possible for your employer and that sometimes your expectations of yourself are unrealistic. Then you can say, "I am learning to ease up on myself and let my employer be the best judge of the quality of my work."

The interview questions could be long and drawn out, and the best way to get through these is to prepare yourself by practicing what you are going to say without sounding rehearsed. Review as many interview-type questions as you can and on a piece of paper note your responses. Compare your responses to your résumé. Are you selling yourself short? Do you really know your own strengths and weaknesses? If you have one handy, use a tape recorder or the recording device on your smartphone to listen to how you sound when speaking. It can be an eye-opener. A video recorder is even more helpful, as you can assess your presentation skills, from the way you sit in a chair to your expression and mannerisms.

1. Do you look poised and professional?
2. How do you use your hands?
3. Are you bright and enthusiastic, or nervous and passive?

Practice, practice, practice a few days before the interview, and correct what you can or ask someone whose opinion you trust to evaluate you. Presumably before attending the interview you have thoroughly read the prerequisites for the position. Your purpose in attending the interview is to confirm in person your suitability for the role. The interviewer will be looking to you for verbal clarification on your suitability and prior experience.

Some companies will set aside time to test your computer skills, so be prepared to undergo some typing tests. If your interview has come about by way of an employment agency, the agency will already have put you through some gruelling tests prior to forwarding your name as a suitable candidate. The agency will not put your name forward for an interview if your skills are not up to par, as they have their own reputation to maintain.

When progressing laterally or advancing within the same organization, you could trump the internal competition by preparing a document that highlights some of your best work, whether it is a PowerPoint presentation that you are especially proud of, a newsletter, or a copy of non-sensitive minutes from a meeting which you personally scribed and prepared. Examples of your work can only enhance your prospects, as it will give the interviewer some insight into your capabilities.

Experience

Earlier in this chapter I touched on the importance of being fully conversant with the content of your résumé. Besides boosting your confidence, having intimate knowledge of your own résumé gives you the opportunity to strongly emphasize your prior achievements while elevating your self-esteem at the same time. Again, lying about prior jobs and experiences is unacceptable, so remember that employers will verify your claims when conducting reference checks.

During the interview, be prepared to talk through the experiences listed on your résumé and what they entailed. Be confident and relaxed, skilfully illustrating to the interviewer that you are comfortable carrying out the job thanks to your previous experience. While describing them, be authentic and speak clearly, describing what you liked most, what you disliked, and why. Make eye contact as much as you can and try not to look down at your hands or out the window. If the interviewer interrupts you frequently, you do not have license to do the same. Never interrupt, and never answer a question that wasn't asked.

A question not to ask, at least in the first interview, is how much they will be paying you. Interviewing protocol dictates that this is in bad taste. If a recruitment agency is acting on your behalf, then they will negotiate salary for you. When representing yourself, put money matters at the very back of your mind because if the company really wants to hire you, the question will come up at the right time, and they will do the asking. When the question does come up, you need to respond with tact. If the position being offered will be your first job, inform the interviewers of this fact. If pressed for a specific figure, confidently request to be compensated at the market rate for the position. If you bring high-calibre expertise to the position, state what you are worth and elaborate on whether your rate is negotiable. That is all you need to think about as far as salary is concerned.

There is a new trend among employers: some companies are requesting within the job advertisements that candidates include salary expectations with their applications. My recommendation when responding to such an advertisement is to state that your salary expectations are reasonable and within the market range, or simply that your salary expectations are negotiable. That way you do not rule yourself out of the process but leave room for further discussion at the interview.

During the course of the interview, you may be asked to describe relationships with former employers. Never discredit a former employer, even if they were the worst boss to have walked this planet. It is just not done, and it instantly brings you down from a potential candidate to a complete undesirable. If any past experience was unpleasant, just speak about your own good qualities and all that you accomplished in that role, ignoring the negative occurrences. You could say, "I respected my boss and worked hard for him, ensuring I always gave my very best effort." Giving such a response gets you away from attempting to concoct a lie. When asked why you plan on leaving your position and employer, never make disparaging remarks such as "I can't stand my boss," "my boss is horrible," or anything along those lines, even if it's true. Instead, talk about the fact that you are seeking career progression, job fulfilment, new challenges and fresh opportunities to enhance your experience. Always take a moment to think before "shooting from the hip" with a response that could cost you the job. Your previous boss's bullying tactics or bad behaviour will eventually come to the surface and be addressed by his own superiors without any requirement for action on your part. In my experience, such behaviour will result in a revolving-door syndrome that eventually becomes evident to others, particularly the decision-makers in the organization, and will be addressed accordingly. If the bad boss has a boss above him, he will want to keep his job and is unlikely to get away with bad behaviour in perpetuity.

The truth of the matter is that although it never gets talked about, people generally leave jobs because they are unhappy with their boss or peers, they don't like the corporate politics, they feel their salary doesn't reflect their value, or they are not being fulfilled, resulting in feelings of hopelessness and de-motivation. The interviewers are just as aware of this fact as you are, but it is not something that gets talked about at an interview. Where secretaries are concerned, 90 percent of the time they will leave for one of the following reasons:

- Sour relationship or personality conflict with boss
- Bullying, disrespectful, or incompetent boss
- Lack of recognition or appreciation
- Lack of job fulfilment
- Unhealthy or hostile work environment
- Intolerable office politics
- Money

Money is usually the least important motivator for a secretary to leave her place of employment, because if all the other areas of her job are positive, the money will come and most experienced secretaries will wait for it. Other mitigating and negative factors such as those mentioned above may help bolster the decision. Most people cite job dissatisfaction as a reason for moving on to greener pastures. Recruiters half expect such a response, but respect and understand that a candidate will never come out and state the truth if it results in denigrating remarks about a past employer. Finally, as you describe your past experiences, be bright and cheerful, and remember that a smile now and again won't hurt.

Good Fit

A friend once made a statement about interviews that I have never forgotten. I had informed her that if I did not get a particular job that I had applied for, I always viewed it as an omen that "it wasn't meant to be." Her reply was interesting. She told me she agreed with that way of thinking to a point but that she also reproached herself by viewing that belief as something of a cop-out. She saw it as a form of justification that helps one live with the fact that she blew the interview, or a clever way of avoiding the unfortunate truth that she simply did not fulfil all the criteria required for the position.

Notably, during the screening process, assessments of all candidates are carried out by a human resources (HR) representative. Depending on the position being applied for, HR, security department personnel, or an external verification company may conduct security checks on potential candidates to ensure they have no criminal records. HR may also verify all educational claims listed on the CV or résumé, carry out reference checks, and may conduct a typing and spelling test as well as a test on the latest word processing software.

One important measure to note is that the HR representative may telephone the candidate to conduct these and other background checks. They prefer to call home telephone numbers as opposed to disturbing a potential candidate at work or putting the candidate in a difficult position by asking her to discuss sensitive matters not related to her present job. As a secretary, please ensure that your voice mail has a professional greeting, because they are likely to judge your telephone skills by that very first call. If you have a greeting that they might deem unprofessional (for example, a pre-recorded response to a radio competition or silly message greetings), they may decide that you are unsuitable, especially if they are looking to fill a senior and prominent role with a polished and professional individual.

Beware of technological and social media pitfalls. The new norm of sharing everything about yourself on Facebook, Twitter, and other social networking sites is fine for socializing but may hinder your professional image and reputation. It is a common occurrence these days for employers to Google potential hires or review postings on social media websites. My advice is never to post anything about yourself that you wouldn't want published on the front page of a national newspaper. Once something is posted on the Internet, you lose control over who views that information and what they do with it. Do not be surprised if a hiring manager or recruiter makes reference to your online profiles as published on various social media platforms, or worse, he simply rules you out of the interview process because of your online reputation.

After a prospective candidate has passed the initial screening process, her name is placed on a short list for the first round of interviews. Initial interviews are an elimination exercise whereby the recruiters narrow down the qualified candidates to those most suitable for the role. Generally, the outcome from the first round of interviews is a short list of three of the best qualified candidates. The second round of interviews usually involves meeting with the hiring manager, otherwise known as your future boss. No matter how impressive a candidate's résumé is or how good she may be with the tests or screening process, the choice of hire ultimately belongs to the hiring manager. If the manager does not feel comfortable with a candidate or doesn't find her a particularly "good fit" despite the HR representative's recommendation, the manager can cherry-pick his or her preferred candidate.

So just how does a manager decide if a candidate is or isn't a good fit? Managers can base this decision on any of the following factors:

1. Do they think they can work with you comfortably five days a week? That is, do you look friendly and approachable, or do you appear aloof, shy, and reserved? If the department involved consists of upbeat extroverts, they may foresee problems.

2. Are you too mature for the rest of the team, which may be comprised of people half your age? If managers envision potential conflicts based on the age gap, they may decide to pass on you for that reason.
3. Do you fit the overall culture at the organization? Being a team player may be of utmost importance in this organization, and perhaps somewhere in your interview you have stressed the fact that you like to work alone. Managers could foresee problems with this.
4. Can you even do the job? If the position requires that you assist the chief executive officer and president, you must be a sharp, intelligent, well-spoken individual who is comfortable communicating with people at all levels of management. You also need to have confidence to spare for that kind of role because you will represent the boss in many situations internally and externally.

If there are any doubts about a candidate's personality or ability to meet the criteria, the company might select a candidate whose personality more closely meets their requirements. Thus, a candidate must "fit" the profile.

When attending an interview, it is imperative to remember that while the company may be interviewing you, you should also be interviewing them. After all, you will be spending thirty to forty hours a week at work on average, and you want to ensure that the environment is a good fit for you as well. If you are uncomfortable or do not like the environment, you have the right to decline the position or subsequent job offer. Try to have your own questions prepared for the interviewers – intelligent questions about issues that matter to you. For instance, you might be interested in working flex hours due to family commitments. It is better to find out before you are hired whether your potential employers support flex hours or job shares. You may also be interested in their benefits structure and whether it meets or exceeds your current one. Vacations may also be important to you, so ask about their vacation policy and how it works.

Another good question to ask is about the dress code, if this is something that is important to you. The interview panel will appreciate these questions. For example, an environment where you could wear jeans any day of the week or casual business attire may not be suitable for someone who prefers to always dress professionally. It would cause that person or their peers to be uncomfortable around each other. This is another dimension to being "a good fit." You must fit in with the corporate culture, the team dynamics, and in some cases the unwritten rules of working in certain organizations. Clear all this up at the interview to eliminate surprises.

Never allow yourself to fret if you are unsuccessful at an interview. Ideally, everyone should be happy to get up every morning and go to work. You do not want to go to a place of work where you will be miserable. It wouldn't be a good fit, and more than likely you would soon be hunting for another job, so try your level best to get it right.

Although my own secretarial career has been fulfilling, I believe I should have planned it a little more carefully to avoid some of the brutal learning curves I have endured, particularly in those instances when I applied for jobs that I had no business applying for – ones that did not advance my career but rather, in some instances, had it going backwards. These were jobs that were not the right fit for my skills or my MMDI (Mental Muscle Diagram Indicator), as defined by Isabel Briggs Myers's personality assessments.[4] Some organizations use psychological assessments to determine personality traits, presented in the form of job demand questionnaires. The assessments are also used to evaluate how a candidate responds to stress in the workplace, what her interpersonal skills are, and the extent to which she is likely to excel or succeed. The results are useful in determining the candidate's suitability for different careers. Psychologists and researchers have various ways of measuring the validity of these tests, and some are considered controversial. I bring this up because I was asked to complete a variety of these personality

4 "Myers-Briggs Widely Used, But Still Controversial," *Psychometric-Success.com*, accessed March 24, 2010, http://www.psychometric-success.com/personality-tests/personality-tests-popular-tests.htm.

assessments in interviews on at least three different occasions. The hiring manager for one interview was very demanding, and the results from the test he required me to take, called the "Fit to Position" Management Assessment Program, were intriguing. I was assessed according to six criteria, or core competencies, in my management profile. Although I found the testing process intense, the outcome was entirely positive and provided me with an opportunity to identify key strengths and developmental opportunities in each of the competency areas. To give you an idea of the type of information a manager might glean from the test and why he might insist that you take one, I have shared my partial results below.[5]

a. *Leadership:* has the capacity to direct and influence others. Establishes and articulates a vision of needed goals and can take decisive action towards attaining those goals.

b. *People management*: works effectively with people in a supervisory and managerial capacity. Is outgoing, understands people, and is able to modify personal style to accomplish objectives.

c. *Interpersonal Relations*: understands the feelings and needs of others; shows a capacity for warmth and tolerance; is outgoing and sociable; seeks out/develops relationships with others.

I discussed my results with the psychologist who assessed me, and she concluded that I was neither an extrovert nor an introvert. My comportment depended on who I was interacting with and the circumstances.

The other tests that I took were vastly different in style and approach and were also carried out for job consideration purposes, but neither opportunity materialized into a job offer. In hindsight, it might be fortunate that it didn't work out, because I was concerned about having a personality conflict with the hiring manager. Ensuring that the personalities are compatible is crucial in any relationship between a boss and his secretary. The right fit for a job is very important for both the

5 HR Management Assessment Program. Test Date: November 8, 2006.

employee and employer, otherwise the working relationship is likely to be very rocky, and no one wants that. Both the employer and employee need to be fully conversant with what each is looking for in the other to ensure a good fit for both parties, and this is why some employers place great emphasis on psychometric tests.

Looking back, I have stayed in some extremely unhealthy work environments for far longer than was necessary, which led me to resent going to work. If you are unhappy at work, ask yourself why and how you can turn that around. If it is a moot point and nothing further can be done to make you enjoy the environment, then clearly it is time to move on. Hence, interviews are extremely important for both sides. If you bear all this in mind at your next interview, you are unlikely to be fazed by the process because you will be cognizant of the fact that it is a two-way street. If it doesn't feel right, you do not have to accept the job, and I would advise you to go with your gut feeling. If you really want the job but do not get it, shed no tears. It's possible that the position isn't what you think it is and isn't suitable for you anyway. Everyone wants to work in the right job with a company where they are valued and wanted, so disappointment is natural when an interview doesn't pan out. Just don't let that stop you from going to the next one!

Motivation

Prior to applying for a position, it is important to get into the habit of asking yourself why you are applying.

- If you saw the posting in an advertisement, why do you feel they should hire you over someone else?
- Does the job function described match your skills?
- Is it a company you have always wanted to work for?
- Are you applying because you are desperate to get a job, any job?
- Is it money that is motivating you?
- If an agency is putting you forward for this position, is this what you really want or just what the agency thinks you want?

In fact, that very question about motivation could come up at an interview and could sway your chances with the interviewer. They could ask what motivates you, and this shouldn't be a question that leaves you dry in the mouth; you should be able to answer it without hesitation. You need to know what motivates you prior to attending an interview because that is the reason you are sitting before the interviewer.

There are many ways to deal with this question, but the foundation of your response should always be honesty. Irrespective of how you choose to respond to the question about what motivates you, it will be apparent to the interviewer if you are being honest or just being politically correct, saying what you think they want to hear. Be honest and you will be respected for it. Try to curb your response if you are motivated purely by money. Never say that you are applying for a job because you heard that the company pays extremely well, and as such you want to work for them. While this might be a part of what motivates you, there ought to be other reasons. If you have none, my suggestion would be to go on the Internet or visit the library and research the company prior to the interview. Find out about the vision for the company, its mission statement, its corporate policy, and its products or services. A stunning response would be to state that the company's corporate values and culture match your own. You could exhibit an interest in their products or services. You could also add that you have heard they are a great company to work for, with high employee satisfaction and low turnover.

Why is it important to identify what motivates you? It makes it easier for you to pinpoint and apply for opportunities that line up well with your own personal goals. Furthermore, if you have mapped out a career path for yourself this will be part of your motivation, that is, progressing in the right direction, and moving towards job satisfaction and career development. Some secretaries are motivated to peak performance only by working in a fast-paced, highly charged environment. In the same situation, others would be overwhelmed. It is therefore important to identify for yourself the right environment for your personality and career goals. Working in an environment that saps your motivation due to demands you find unacceptable is unhealthy and unlikely to yield favourable results for either side, while another candidate could thrive in such an environment. Know what motivates you!

Availability

When you score top marks in an interview, the company looking to hire you will likely wait if you are unavailable to commence with them right away. However, it is important to note that sometimes you can lose a position simply because a company may require an individual to start immediately and might be unable and unwilling to wait for someone to serve their notice with their present employer. This is rare, but it can happen. If the company is dealing with an employment agency, the agency could send a "temp" to cover the position until you are able to start. However, during the course of my career, I have seen positions posted where it was a requirement that the successful individual be available to start immediately. I have also lost positions where I was short-listed with another candidate who was available to start right away when I wasn't. In other words, you can be overlooked simply because of restrictions on your availability. This hardly seems fair, but it is worth noting, as it does happen now and again.

Sometimes, once a company becomes aware that you are leaving, they pay you to leave in lieu of notice if they are equally keen to get rid of you. Should this occur, it might be prudent to advise your new employer just in case they would rather you started immediately. However, a small breather between jobs can do you a world of good. It is best to take on a venture such as starting a new job poised and refreshed.

Figure 5 - Sample Interview Questions

Interviewers will pose well-crafted questions in an effort to establish your suitability for the role. Below are some questions frequently asked during interviews:

1. Can you tell me a little bit about yourself/your educational background?
2. Why are you looking for a new position? Why did you leave or are you planning to leave your current position?
3. What do you enjoy most about your current role, and what do you enjoy the least?
4. With respect to your current/previous position, what accomplishment are you most proud of?
5. What would you say was your biggest disappointment in your previous position?
6. What do you know about our company?
7. If hired, what would be your first objective in your new role?
8. What do you suppose your current employer would identify as your greatest strengths? What about areas of improvement?
9. How do you normally react when someone is critical of your work?
10. Would you rather have structure or flexibility in a job?
11. What are your short-term career goals (two years)? What steps have you taken so far to achieve these?
12. What are your long-term goals (five years)?
13. You have changed jobs frequently. Do you plan on moving around a lot throughout your career?
14. What are your hobbies outside of work?
15. Do you have any questions for us?

The sample interview questions in Figure 5 represent some of the most prevalent questions to come up in an interview. Most seasoned interviewees go into an interview half expecting these staple interview questions. However, even the most seasoned interviewee makes mistakes. Even with all of my knowledge in this area I still managed to greatly embarrass myself at one interview for a very prominent position. I was slated to attend interviews with two different reputable firms two days apart, and I got my facts mixed up in my response to the question, "What do you know about our company?" With the interview itself progressing extremely well, the CEO of one of the firms proceeded to ask me, "What specifically on our website impressed you about our firm?" I suddenly had a brain freeze as I tried to isolate the facts about this particular firm from those of the other I had been learning about. There was a long, very awkward silence as I struggled to determine which fact belonged to which firm. I finally responded with what I later learned was an incorrect remark that was about the other firm. Immediately after giving my response to the CEO, the atmosphere in the room changed. There was no mistaking the huge cloud of disappointment that swept over his face. Later that evening at home, after realizing my mistake, I wrote to thank him for his time and acknowledged the factual error. The CEO was kind enough to reply to my e-mail, thanking me for "clearing things up." It came as no surprise to me when I received the rejection letter from that firm a few days later. A classic case of self-sabotage! You do not want to make the same mistake as I did, so prepare for and attend just *one interview at a time.*

Some companies prefer to use the aforementioned STAR interview criteria, which is a series of questions used to determine or predict future behaviour based on past actions. Behavioural-type interviews are more in depth and typically require a situation and resolution type of response to the interviewer's questions. The interviewer asks the candidate to recall a prior situation or event that occurred in the workplace. He or she then asks the candidate to set the scenario and give a detailed explanation of the steps taken to remedy the situation and the final outcome. Most behavioural-type questions follow a theme or particular focus. It is important for candidates to be prepared for the occurrence of a behavioural-based interview. Figure 6 in this chapter highlights some examples of questions that an interviewer might place emphasis on.

Figure 6 - Behavioural (STAR)–Based Interview Questions

A. Good Fit

Describe a situation where you feel you demonstrated your strengths in interpersonal relationships, particularly with respect to your manager or supervisor. What possible negative outcomes do you feel you thwarted by being supportive?

B. Organizational and Prioritizing Skills

Tell me (us) about a time when you were asked to handle more than one task at the same time. How did you prioritize and organize your time and workload? What was the outcome?

C. Teamwork

Give me (us) an example or situation where you had to work as part of a team to accomplish a task. What was the task and how many people were in the group? What difficulties arose as a result of working as a group? What role did you play in resolving these difficulties? How successful was the group in completing the task?

D. Interpersonal Relationships

Tell me (us) about a time when you had to deal with challenging personalities in a demanding work environment. Give me (us) an example of an incident and the outcome.

E. Communication

Tell me (us) about a time when you had to create a written communiqué or relay an important message to someone. How did you go about doing so, and what mode did the communiqué take? Take me (us) through the steps you took to ensure that the message was relayed correctly. What precautions did you take to ensure that the message was not misconstrued by anyone? What was the outcome?

F. Customer Service

Give me (us) an example of what you consider to be your best customer service occurrence in the workplace.

G. Performance

Tell me (us) about a time when your boss was particularly pleased with your performance. What were the steps you took to ensure that you met and exceeded his expectations?

Interview Preparation: A Day-by-Day Checklist for Interview Preparation

Two days before ...

1. Go on the Internet and conduct research on the company. Find out as much as you can about the company's history, services or products, corporate vision, culture, number of employees, and department you might be working in.
2. Check the location of the office and determine how to get there. If uncertain, contact the company's receptionist for directions and approximate travel time.
3. On paper, clarify to yourself your expectations from the position and why you are interested in working for the company. Would accepting the position be in line with your career goals?
4. On paper, write down your strengths and weaknesses.
5. Gather some common interview questions and do a practice session with a friend or someone you trust and respect, or practice your responses in front of a mirror or use an audio/video recorder.
6. Be prepared to respond to some behavioural-type questions.
7. Make two extra copies of your résumé to take with you to the interview in case the panel is short a copy.
8. Make copies of your reference list to take with you to the interview.

9. If available, take some examples of your past work, as long as they do not compromise your confidentiality agreement with a current or previous employer.
10. If possible, go and have a manicure done the day before.

The night before …

1. Determine how you are going to get to the interview site and ensure that you have made the appropriate arrangements to get there on time.
2. Determine what you are going to wear and examine it to make sure it's in good condition. Be sure that your garments are clean, ironed, and appropriate for the interview. Is your clothing suitable for a business setting? Whenever you are uncertain about what to wear for an interview, err on the formal side, or consult with an image consultant several days prior.
3. Your shoes should be polished, shined, and in good condition. You can be certain that by the time you exit the interview room, someone will definitely have looked at your shoes.
4. Is your jewellery excessive?
    a. For men: a classic or decent watch, wedding band (if married), and cufflinks are all acceptable.
    b. For women: a simple watch, wedding and engagement ring (if married), plus simple stud earrings are all you will need. If you have to wear a necklace, it should be worn under your shirt or blouse. However, a simple strand of pearls is acceptable if it goes with your outfit or matches your earrings. Other forms of jewellery such as clanking bangles and bracelets, big dangling earrings, and oversized necklaces should definitely be avoided.
5. Place all your documents in a professional portfolio ready for your trip.
6. Take your mind off the interview itself and just relax.
7. If your interview is early in the morning, go to bed early and get plenty of sleep in order to be bright and alert when you need to be.

The day of…

1. Before leaving home, check your appearance in a full-length mirror, and do not forget to check the view from the back. The simple exercise of ensuring that your presentation is immaculate before stepping out of your home not only boosts your confidence but also increases your chances of passing the "first impression" test.
2. Practice good grooming. Keep your hair neat, tidy, and professional, and remember that you do not want your hair or clothes to detract from your presentation.
3. The rules of etiquette state you should always ensure that those around you are comfortable. Having a button missing on your shirt, an unravelling hemline, or an unkempt appearance is not only careless, but it makes others uncomfortable, and as such it is not good etiquette.
4. Avoid plying yourself with heavy perfume or aftershave.

Twenty minutes before …

1. Arrive at the building at least fifteen minutes early. That extra fifteen minutes will help to calm your nerves and prepare you for the interview as opposed to rushing in late and flustered.
2. You should enter the building itself at least ten minutes prior to your pre-set interview time. Promptness will be looked upon favourably. Being even five minutes late is unacceptable and unprofessional.
    a. If, however, something serious does crop up causing you to be late, do not wait until the last minute to let them know, if you can help it. Phone ahead and speak to whoever your contact is and advise them of your situation.
    b. If you are attending the interview via an employment agency, then you need to phone the agency and they will get in touch with their client and apologize on your behalf.
3. Turn off your mobile phone or any other communication device.
4. Ensure that your palms are not sweaty or sticky with hand cream.

During the interview ...

1. Make your winning entrance by walking into the interviewing room with your head held high and with all the confidence that you can muster.
2. As the introductions are made, the interviewers will want to shake hands with you. Extend your right hand and with a strong, firm grip, grasp the other person's whole hand (not just the fingers), shake once, and then release.
3. Wait until the panel has sat down before doing so yourself. In fact, wait for them to invite you to sit down and they will motion to you precisely where they would like you to sit.
4. If you are seated in an open forum, sit erect and if you choose to cross your legs at the knees, do not persistently cross and uncross your legs. You can also sit simply with your legs and feet together or one foot slightly in front of the other. For women in particular, never cross your legs at the ankle, especially when sitting at an open forum, as this simply isn't an elegant position and conveys a certain uneasiness or nervousness.
5. Make eye contact with everyone on the interview panel and *smile.*
6. When asked a question, keep an open expression on your face and try not to frown if the question surprises or even infuriates you. Instead, smile, and then proceed to answer the question as honestly as you can.
7. Speak clearly and concisely, maintaining eye contact with the interviewer. If there is more than one interviewer, do not concentrate on one and alienate the other – address everyone in the room.
8. Exercise good listening skills. If you do not understand a question, ask for clarification. If you cannot answer a question because you do not know the answer, or you have never encountered the situation posed to you, simply tell the truth. If you endeavour to make up a story in order to impress – the interviewers will see right through you. Simply state that you

have never encountered such a situation and offer a suggestion as to how you would handle it if it did come up.

9. When asked a question in the interview, never answer in monosyllables such as yes or no and leave it at that.
10. When you have fully answered the question, stop talking and wait for the next question.
11. Be careful not to over-answer a question either. Be confident in your knowledge and don't ramble, answering the question in many different ways; it isn't necessary. The recruiter or interviewer is not obtuse. Your interviewers get it, and they understood you the first time.
12. Never chew gum or fidget nervously with a pen, paper, or your hands. This indicates nervousness and lack of confidence.
13. Minimize gesturing with your hands as much as possible. In some of my past interviews where I found myself gesturing with my hands, I observed the recruiter's eyes following my hands up and down and sideways. You do not want that to happen.

After the interview …

1. It is perfectly acceptable to send a thank-you note to the interviewer(s) in the form of an e-mail or thank-you card, but do keep it short, expressing only your appreciation for being afforded the opportunity to interview for the position and that you look forward to joining the company should you be the successful candidate.
2. Avoid telephone calls as a follow-up method unless invited to do so, or you could permanently write yourself off from the position.

    a. However, if some weeks have gone by and you have not had a response or letter indicating the company's position regarding your interview, you may telephone the recruiting manager to inquire as to whether they have filled the position or if they are still considering you. In the event that they are still reviewing their options, they will appreciate your call and may reconsider you on account of your exhibited enthusiasm. A keen candidate is always preferred to one that is aloof. I was successful in landing a position many years ago in London, England, on account of my follow-up telephone call. The successful candidate had suddenly withdrawn her candidacy and declined the job offer made to her. By sheer happenstance, I called in at the right moment and they hired me instead.

Summary

- Read job descriptions thoroughly and be certain that your skills match the employer's needs.
- Once you submit your application and are subsequently invited to attend an interview, you must do your research about the company.
- Ask yourself the important questions about what you can bring to the organization and why they should pick you over another candidate.
- Be prepared to talk about your past experiences with confidence and enthusiasm.
- Never discredit any past employers in an interview; it serves no purpose and ultimately ruins your chances of being hired.
- Interviews are a two-way street, so prepare to interview the prospective employer by asking all the questions that are important to you.
- Know what motivates you. This not only aids in your choice of jobs to apply for but also helps you determine your ideal career environment.
- Prior to attending the interview, be clear about your availability and whether it is flexible.
- If available, review a variety of sample interview questions in preparation for your interview.
- Prepare an interview checklist for yourself that takes into account the period leading up to, during, and after the interview.
- Address issues about appropriate dress at least a week prior to the interview date.
- If an interview doesn't work out for you, move on to the next job prospect and apply the same strategy until you get the right opportunity – one that aligns with your own personal goals and career aspirations.

Chapter 4: New Kid on the Block

The first week on a new job can be at the same time tough and exciting, depending on the nature of your job and who you will be working for. If you are starting on the bottom rung and working for someone who is not a "higher-up" in the company, don't be all that surprised if you are treated with a little less respect than you feel should be your due. However, if you make yourself indispensable to this individual, you may soon find a change in his attitude. When it comes down to it, few people understand or make any real attempt to care about the true role of a secretary. The majority of those bosses who are lucky enough to have a secretary don't really know how to use this invaluable resource. There really is no manual or book that teaches someone who has never had a secretary precisely how to maximize that privilege. This is something that you will quietly observe if you are astute.

Often, as a general secretary in a conventional office, you will be introduced to all the members of your team within your department on your very first day. Also on that first day, you will most likely meet the rest of the staff and the company managers. Introductions are done on the first day in most firms, and depending on the size of the organization they are done in person or via a broadcast memorandum to the company, or both communication channels may be used. If a broadcast memorandum is issued, typically via e-mail, the announcement will be in the form of a brief bio informing your new peers about your qualifications, area of expertise, previous employer, and any other highlights worth mentioning. The person formulating the communiqué to the company may or may not seek your input (ideally they should at least consult you, but this doesn't always happen); whether they do or not doesn't really matter, as this is a mere formality. People soon forget what is on paper, but they do tend to remember their first impression of you and what you tell them. Since you are a newcomer, people will want you to be aware of who they are and their position in the company.

A honeymoon phase will ensue in which assistance will be readily available, but that soon passes, and at some stage you, as a new employee, will be expected to figure things out on your own. Some employers make a point of indicating their preference for "self-starters" in job advertisements to lessen this learning curve. Self-starters are people who are able to hit the ground running upon hire, and a request for one means the company prefers someone who is self-sufficient and capable of immediately getting on with the job with minimal assistance and/or supervision.

If you are starting out as a junior secretary the learning curve is often extended, and all your work is supervised by a senior administrative person. At a junior level, this is to be expected. Your goal ought to be to learn as much as you can from those more experienced than you. As the junior secretary, you will most likely be assigned to assist a number of managers. If you are good at your job, this is noticed very early on and a manager or director may snap you up to be his or her personal secretary. Most junior secretaries, if they are very good, remain junior for no more than two to three years, then move on or get promoted. It is all about progression and is perfectly acceptable.

You will have learned from secretarial school or previous jobs that within each organization there's a chain of command. On your very first day, if it is not handed to you by your immediate supervisor or whoever is orienting you into the organization, you must request a copy of the organizational chart. As a newcomer, you will eventually learn and understand the chain of command within your organization. However, your initial concern must be cantered on learning who is who so that you can perform your tasks efficiently.

A more experienced and senior secretary is generally not afforded much of a learning curve. Most bosses in the higher echelons of management have very high expectations, and a new secretary at this level will usually be expected to figure things out for herself and get on with the job at hand. At this level, the secretary will understand the process involved in getting acclimatized to a new company and position, and she will make a point of seeking out and becoming aware of the power players in the company.

The onus is on the newcomer to make a positive first impression during her first few days, weeks and months at a new company. As a secretary, irrespective of your level of experience, you must convey some or all of the following attributes in order to garner that good first impression and make it last:

- Poise
- Confidence
- Friendly disposition
- Professionalism
- Common Sense

Poise

Poise is a kind of calm, self-assured dignity combined with elegance and gracefulness, and those considered to possess these attributes are often referred to as "polished" individuals.

You convey poise by your deportment and demeanour, meaning the way that you carry and present yourself overall. Polished individuals almost always give a good first impression and, in some cases, have a commanding presence about them. They exude elegance of manner and refinement.

You will know whether you have poise by observing how people respond to you; in some cases they will tell you. However, polished professionals know that they are viewed this way without the ego-boosting accolades. It is a certain way of being that is innate, and although it's difficult to describe, it stems from one's upbringing and educational background. Polished individuals are well mannered, well spoken, cultured, refined, composed, and calm, with a certain air of confidence about them and an ability to handle themselves well in any given situation.

If you don't have poise and would like to, experience, confidence, and acceptance of who you are is a good way to start. If you wish to acquire the much sought-after trait, there are a couple of things that can get you there. First of all, start by observing those who do have poise – their mannerisms, the way they speak, their aura, and their general presentation. It is easy to spot someone with poise. You find yourself constantly staring at them and quietly admiring everything about them. You also find that people are drawn to them and they always appear at ease within themselves and around others. Observation is the first step towards polishing your own appearance. There's a second way to develop poise, if you feel you need it. You can attend deportment or life-coaching classes, where you are taught how to behave like a lady or gentleman. In some countries these courses are referred to as finishing schools. An accumulation of some secretarial experience and targeted refinement in other areas of your social behaviour will interweave this rare trait into your persona.

Confidence

To be an efficient secretary you must be able to converse with anyone at any level, whether internal or external to the organization, with unbridled self-confidence. Confidence is not arrogance or an expression of a feeling of self-importance to others. Rather, confidence comes from a sense of self-worth, an aura of self-assurance, and an inner sense of integrity. Never confuse confidence with arrogance. Arrogant people are driven by their ego and a kind of superciliousness. They are poor listeners, swellheaded, and love to talk about themselves. Arrogant people are abrasive and condescending, with a tendency to look down on others.

Confidence goes hand in hand with poise, although many confident people are not "polished." When you are comfortable with your abilities and know that you are the right candidate for the position, then typically you are confident. That confidence translates into how you carry yourself and communicate.

During an interview, if you are not confident it will be apparent in your composure, style of communication, and delivery of your message. Confidence cannot be learned. Rather, it just becomes a part of your personality depending on various factors, such as your prior experience, self-belief, education, knowledge of your subject matter, and the environment you are in. Confidence does come with experience. The more experienced you are as a secretary, the more confident you will be in your abilities.

Friendly Disposition

When you are new on the job, you will want to appear approachable and friendly. If you are genuine and warm, people will reciprocate and may even go out of their way to help ease your first day/ week/month jitters. However, there are certain kinds of people that one encounters who enjoy making newcomers in a work environment nervous and uneasy. If you go in aware of this, you will not be easily intimidated, and when you are self-assured and confident, it will not be an issue for you. Some of the people you will be introduced to will appear unfriendly and uninterested, but if you can still maintain a friendly disposition you won't antagonize them, and with any luck, they will soon be on your side.

One tip I have found useful in my past experiences has been to write people's names down as soon as they have been introduced to me. This does not mean that as soon as someone is introduced to you, you start scribbling away in front of her. Rather, make a mental note of her name, title, and physical characteristics and then when you return to your desk or as she walks away from you, quickly jot down this information and anything else that can help you to remember who she is. For instance,

Mary Winstanley

-Financial Controller

-Round face, short curly brown hair, blue eyes, tall and slim

Geoffrey Toole

-Mail room clerk

-Medium height, jet black hair, navy-blue uniform, nice smile

The next time you encounter these individuals you will gain their respect and support simply by remembering their names and knowing exactly who they are. They will be very impressed if you greet them by name with genuine enthusiasm, despite having met a large number of people in the company within a short space of time.

Being the new kid on the block can be daunting and uncomfortable, but the degree to which you feel this largely depends on your personality. If you are robust, intuitive, and have a proactive type-A personality, you will probably settle in quite quickly. You will endear some peers to you and equally aggravate others, like anything in life. This brings up a very important point. Know going in that not everyone is going to like you. As soon as you meet some people they will exhibit unfriendly mannerisms towards you. Others will immediately launch a campaign that either attempts to discredit your integrity or find a way to spotlight your weaknesses. Typically this is done by certain unsavoury personalities who are highlighted later in this chapter; they are driven to this kind of behaviour by a personal agenda that only they understand. Thus a strong characteristic for a secretary to have is the ability to keep a level head and remain unfazed by challenging personalities. You must be able to shrug these people and their actions off and realize that it is not really about you as much as it is about them. You will make some friends very quickly, but keep these liaisons strictly professional, particularly if you have a sensitive role, for example if you are secretary to the CEO, CFO, president, or executive vice president.

Secretaries who are new to the field might be intimidated by those known as "office bullies," and experience will teach you that they are everywhere. When you leave school you assume that you leave the world of bullying behind, but you will find another one waiting for you in the workplace, and there is no point in running away because there will nearly always be one wherever you go. If there are no outright bullies, there will at least be unpleasant people to be around. Learn early on in your career to display an air of calm despite the circumstances, and you will be able to face any challenging situation as your experience and confidence grow. Never compromise your spiritual and ethical beliefs in order to endear yourself to another person; you will be doing both parties a disservice. Know who you are and don't change to please someone else. The only person you really have to worry about is your boss. Even then, remember who you are and ensure that your values are never compromised. Your boss will respect you for it.

Seasoned secretaries working with bullies in their midst should note the following:

1. Office bullies act out their insecurities by being malicious to those that they most admire or revere.
2. Bullies are cowards when confronted about their behaviour or actions by an equally strong and imposing personality.
3. Sometimes the bully can end up being your boss (see chapter 9 for suggestions on countering such behaviour from the person writing your paycheck).
4. Bullying tactics can appear in many forms, so it gives newcomers the upper hand if they can recognize these tactics and their intent before reacting.

The rules of this game can be different where male secretaries are concerned. As long as they continue to be a novelty in this profession, their experience will be starkly different from that of female secretaries. Male secretaries are less likely to fall prey to the office bully, particularly female office bullies, simply because women tend to be very catty towards one another and more amicable with men. A male secretary whom I interviewed for this book described himself as the "fly on the wall" in his office. The female secretary contingent in his office engage in tittle-tattle about other female colleagues and typically forget that he is present or within earshot of their gossip-fest. He believes that they think he is harmless or simply forget that he is also a secretary with his own feelings and opinions. He said that he is often tempted to embarrass them greatly by revealing all they've said to the subject of their gossip. According to this male secretary and others that I interviewed, the unsavoury personality types that I highlight in this chapter are accurate.

Professionalism

On your first day, try to maintain your professionalism by assuming a collaborative work style. This helps the existing team feel comfortable about welcoming you into the fold, and it also earns you immediate respect. Arrive on time for work. In fact, find out what time your immediate boss normally arrives for work, and try to arrive fifteen minutes to half an hour earlier. If, however, your boss arrives at an ungodly hour or earlier than what is normally deemed to be early and it is impossible to compete, then simply aiming to arrive between fifteen and thirty minutes prior to your start time displays professionalism. Naturally there are days when you will be late due to traffic or other eventualities, and as long as this doesn't become the norm, you need not worry too much about that affecting your punctuality record. If you work with reasonable people, occasional lateness shouldn't be held against you, because some days it will happen due to no fault of your own. Again, do not make it a perpetual habit so that your tardiness is what you are known for in the office. Overall you need to do what is comfortable for you within the bounds of professionalism. If you must negotiate a different start time with your boss due to personal reasons such as taking the kids to school, issues with traffic every morning, or transportation to work, that is fine, as long as you remain consistent.

Your telephone manners also demonstrate your level of professionalism. Maintain a pleasant and professional tone when you are speaking on the telephone, and the pleasantness of your voice will reach whomever you are talking to. Answer the telephone politely with clarity and confidence and you will be perceived as possessing such. Ensure that your voice mail greeting on your telephone is professional and in line with the corporation's guidelines. (Study the "Telephone Etiquette" guidelines in chapter 7 of this book.)

As the newcomer, greet everyone you encounter, and if you remember their names, greet them by name. If you see a strange face within your work environment, take a moment to introduce yourself. Extending yourself in that way will earn you respect and a warm welcome into the fold. The manager or your immediate supervisor will attempt to introduce you to as many people as he possibly can at any given time, but not everyone who works for the company may be present on that day or even where they are supposed to be. Others may be missed on the introductory tour as well, so recognize that you are the stranger and that the onus is on you to ensure you are welcome in the new environment; this is the best tack to take.

Common Sense

Common sense in this context simply means avoiding acting without thinking. Your employer or boss expects common sense and intelligent interaction with clients and peers. Depending on your level of seniority – that is, if you are a junior or senior secretary – a certain mature approach to your interactions with internal and external customers is expected right from day one, especially if you work independently and unsupervised. Stupid and costly mistakes will never be erased from your boss's mind and may hinder your growth potential within the firm.

The employer trusts that you will manage your time wisely, treat everyone around you with dignity and respect, know when to interrupt a meeting and when not to, use initiative in dealing with minor issues, and most importantly, handle the requirements of your position with minimal direction or supervision. It is at the early stages after you are hired that employers observe your level of common sense and suitability for the role. The probationary period is generally imposed for this purpose and is a good opportunity for successful candidates to prove their worth.

Every manager who hires a secretary does so with the expectation that the secretary will ease his workload and ultimately make his work life easier. The key traits associated with the successful secretary's approach to her role are

- Attention to detail
- Discretion
- Dependability
- Discipline
- Determination

Other helpful characteristics that demonstrate your common sense as you execute your tasks are

- Competency
- Intuitiveness
- Logic

Irrespective of your level of experience, common sense, pragmatism, and the ability to communicate well are essential qualities, and when it is discernible to the rest of the team that you are level-headed, their confidence in your abilities will manifest itself.

From the moment you learn that you are the successful candidate, plan how you are going to conduct yourself during the first day/first week/first month. For instance, decide how you are going to encourage and build positive relationships within your new team, how you are going to organize yourself and your new manager, how you will establish smart, meaningful processes for the department, and how you are going to improve your manager's work life. These are goals that you need to set for yourself whether you are a novice or a highly skilled and experienced secretary.

Being the new kid on the block does get easier, but it can be a daunting and exhausting process. We have all experienced "being new" at some stage in our lives – the experience of being the new person in an organization is no different than being the new kid at school. To accelerate the process of transitioning from a newcomer to an insider, you are the one who has to make that extra effort. Most employers will help their new secretaries through the transition process to fit in by making them feel comfortable and allowing them the time they need to go through the learning curve. However, in some organizations, as much as the boss may wish to do so, the stress and pressure of his position may hinder that extended helpfulness, and your progression will depend on your own resilience.

A secretary who resolves crises and finds answers to her own questions without being spoon-fed is a great asset and has the makings of that "super-elite secretary" every manager seeks. Managers do not want a secretary who constantly needs to be managed and who becomes part of the problem rather than the solution. Demonstrate your common sense by taking initiative and researching further the mission, values, and goals of the organization. Still, you will need to be aware of your own limitations when you are new and know when to ask for help if and when it is warranted.

As soon as you become a member of the organization, you would be wise to study as much as you can about the company on its Intranet (the internal section of the website that is not open to the general public). Familiarize yourself with company procedures and policies, key personnel in certain areas, and the latest company news and announcements issued via press releases. Pick up company brochures and any other literature you can find to educate yourself about the company. Within your own division, your boss should guide you. However, if he is the ultra-busy type, you may have to buy coffee for one of your colleagues and take advantage of the meeting to get answers to any questions you may have. It is a rare occurrence but one that is advantageous to you when your predecessor makes herself available to show you the ropes.

Another source of helpful information is the files that you will no doubt manage for your boss. As long as you remain ethical in your review of them, you can learn a lot about major company operations and customers. Be patient with the learning process. Never join a company with the intention of being a superwoman or super-secretary. Your goal in the first few months ought to be to learn at a steady pace. It is impossible to amass a year's worth of knowledge in one day; it will take about that long before you are truly comfortable in your new job and graduate from the status of a newcomer.

Do remember that asking for guidance and acknowledging that you do not know the answer to a certain question is a sign of common sense; it is better to do this instead of being a "Miss Know-It-All" who then proceeds to get things wrong. Clarify your understanding by repeating and confirming what you are told. The other party will appreciate it.

As you make friends within the company and cultivate working relationships with members of your immediate team, you will begin to understand their roles within the organization and how they affect your position. Sometimes when a new candidate joins a team, the existing members may take advantage of the fact that this person is willing to do anything to fit in. You may be asked to perform certain tasks that are awkward and make you feel extremely uncomfortable. You can find yourself caught up in real ethical dilemmas. When this situation occurs, talk to your boss to ensure that whatever action you are about to take does not compromise any particular principle of the corporation's ethics or your own.

Unsavoury Office Personalities

There are a variety of methods that psychologists use to identify and categorize personality types. One of them is the psychological test, which measures an individual's personality or temperament.

- The aforementioned Myers-Briggs Type Indicator® (MBTI) is one instrument that is widely used for measuring personality types and preferences. According to the Myers and Briggs Foundation website, "the purpose of the Myers-Briggs Type Indicator® (MBTI) personality inventory is to make the theory of psychological types described by C. G. Jung understandable and useful in people's lives." The MBTI® was developed by the eminent psychologist Isabel Myers Briggs and her mother, Katherine Briggs.[6]
- Another method is the widely used Type A and Type B personality theory which, distinguishes between two extremes

6 "MBTI Basics," *Myers Briggs.org,* accessed March 14, 2010, http://www.myersbriggs.org/my-mbti-personality-type/mbti-basics.

– the aggressive personality type (extrovert) and the placid personality type (introvert).

- There is also the popular True Colours® personality profiling tool. Considered to be highly effective, the tool assigns four colours to four distinct personality types, principally based on analogous traits and attributes.

There are, no doubt, many more personality tests. Regardless, over the course of your career you will undoubtedly encounter difficult people. They will come in a variety of personalities and will be obnoxious to different degrees. Due to the subordinate nature of the secretarial role, secretaries often bear the brunt of these office ogres.

For this book, I have chosen to assign labels to these problem co-workers that resonate with anyone who has ever worked in an office, *especially secretaries.*

The Fault-Finder

This is the kind of person who never compliments you when you do a good job but who is very quick to point out your mistakes. No matter how efficient you may be, this individual focuses on your errors and never your accomplishments. Quite often, the fault-finder is that one person in the office with whom you have a direct personality conflict. They typically enjoy pointing out any and all of your mistakes to you and everyone else for some perverse sense of personal gratification. They also love to tell others that you are not a team player, simply because they have a frosty relationship with you. They jump to conclusions and make incorrect assumptions because they are so hung up on discrediting you that they never bother to get the whole story before accusing you of making a mistake. Unfortunately, the fault-finder can be your boss. When this happens, you simply have to learn to live with it, and use the fault-finding episodes as a challenge to make as few mistakes as possible. A number of secretaries described experiences with people they labelled as "office fault-finders," and it was a revelation for me because I thought they were unique to my own experience. My own method of dealing and coping with such individuals was to shrug it off and counter their behaviour with the opposite reaction. If indeed I was in the wrong, I simply acknowledged their observation, thanked them, and promised to rectify the matter. I tried to remain calm, cool, and unflustered – the antithesis of their confrontational behaviour.

The Gossipmonger

Engaging in office gossip can be irresistible. Inevitably, even those of us who know better can find ourselves entangled in some juicy office gossip. By this label for a personality type, please note that I am referring to people whose behaviour is extreme, and not to those who simply take part in the gossip mill. Much like the office bully, gossipmongers deflect attention from themselves by making it their business to spread vicious rumours about others, particularly those that they secretly admire. These people cannot and should not be trusted with sensitive or private information. If you become aware that you are the subject of vile and untrue gossip, you need to address and eliminate the rumours with the help of your human resources department or your boss, or else you must confront the perpetrator directly. Gossipmongers are not averse to making up stories and being creative with the truth if the opportunity presents itself.

Do your part when the shoe is on the other foot; that is, when you are the one inclined to engage in or instigate office tittle-tattle – refrain from such behaviour, as it is hurtful, childish, and unnecessary.

The Inquisitor

These people make it their business to find out everything about their peers to satisfy a driving curiosity that forms a part of their personality. While you should never be rude to inquiring minds, be firm about what you will or won't divulge about yourself. Inquisitive work colleagues can be quite persistent in their quest to learn everything they possibly can about others. They typically aren't satisfied when the response is lacking in details. To stop whatever you consider to be an intrusive line of questioning, respond politely by disclosing only what you deem necessary, and then turn the very same question on them: "Well, how about you? Tell me about yourself!" Quite often they are thrown off by that question because they are so nosy about other people's affairs that they have no interest in talking about themselves.

A friend once warned me not to disclose too much about myself to work colleagues because, as he stated, they could and *would* use that information against me. I must say that his words had gravitas, because that scenario has played itself out now and again in my own career. During my working life in England, the mere act of saying, "Hello, how do you do?" was not interpreted as an invitation to share one's life story. Rather, the greeter typically expected an affirmative response and nothing more, with no extra details required. In comparison, my work experience in North America proved to be the most difficult for me, as I experienced horror at the intrusive and probing questions that were bandied about. Even at the time this book was published, I was still truly dumbfounded by the lack of sophistication and blatant intrusion into matters that I consider personal and private. For example, I have had work colleagues blatantly ask me why I was not married. One colleague quizzed me about my vacation, wanting to know who I went with, a man or a girlfriend.

If you can help it, disclose only what you want to share with your peers and colleagues, and change the subject about anything that is really none of their business. Be warned that inquisitive people love to collect information about others, and worst of all, they find it difficult to sit on that information, so they usually end up sharing it.

The Manipulator

Beware of this type of individual. Manipulators wear many faces and exhibit "Jekyll and Hyde" tendencies. They are usually driven by an unhealthy and unrealistic desire to be better than everyone else at anything and everything. Manipulators are very competitive – everything they do is about sizing up their competition and determining how they can win. They will use their many faces to suit any situation and will deflect any negativity attributed to them or their actions. Their goal is to be the leader of the pack, respected and admired by everyone in the office, and they are very good at manipulating any situation to their benefit. They are quick to shift blame or negative feedback onto someone else. Manipulators are experts at ingratiating themselves with superiors or anyone else they want to impress, and yet as soon as that person leaves the room, their true colours emerge. These individuals are always playing mind games; hence, I label them "manipulators." Most are good at fooling others into believing that they are indeed the person they appear to be.

The Slacker

This is the office busybody who gets nothing done, always walking around aimlessly and chitchatting with anyone who will listen. Slackers are not confrontational at all; indeed, they tend to be very personable and likeable. The issue with slackers is that they are fun people to be around and usually mean no harm, but quite often you have to ask them more than once to complete a task before they take any kind of action. Even if this is the case, it is neither your place nor your business as the newcomer to point this out to the boss or anyone else. The powers that be are not blind, and quite possibly they have a good reason for not interfering. They could be engaging in their own observation exercise of the staff member's behaviour, which may eventually lead to a showdown or loss of employment. Stay out of it and just focus on your own workload.

The Office Flirt

Flirts exhibit behaviour much like the slackers. Their sole intention is to flirt with those they are either attracted to or from whom they seek favours. Flirts treat the office as a playground, where they can ingratiate themselves to whomever they choose. Sometimes the flirtatious behaviour is used to gain ground on someone else in the office politics at the firm. At other times it is used to gain favours from targeted individuals who have influence. Flirts also like to be the centre of attention. Engaging in a conversation with one is an exercise in patience, as they always find a way to bring the topic back to themselves. Indeed, flirts are harmless because they are so self-absorbed. The flirt is not always immediately apparent to you as a newcomer, but in time you can pick the flirt out of the flock. All you can do in this scenario is watch with amusement, then ignore the behaviour and leave it alone.

The Passive-Aggressive Co-worker

Passive-aggressive people engage in behaviour that is designed to intimidate their chosen subjects. They do this by deliberately giving you the cold shoulder or purposely ignoring you in a manner that makes you notice the snub. What is interesting about this group is the underlying reason behind their passive-aggressiveness. Quite often it is due to an inferiority complex. If the passive-aggressive person is someone on your immediate team or even your boss, you must address how they make you feel without being confrontational. You could simply ask them if things are all right between the two of you, or if there is an issue that needs to be addressed. If you do this it is unlikely that they will tell you why they are behaving this way towards you, but it might just make them stop. Never respond in kind to passive-aggressive people; instead, embarrass them by being nice. The passive-aggressiveness may stop if it doesn't appear to be working.

The Show-off

Yes, these people exist in all walks of life, including the office environment. Show-offs are also known as "know-it-alls" or "drama queens" and have an inflated ego along with a firm belief that they are never wrong. They are always schmoozing with those in positions of power. As the new kid on the block, you may find yourself the target of the office show-offs and other extremely loud personalities. The show-offs cannot help themselves; they find it difficult to withhold any type of information, whether it is personal or business. They love to create drama that puts the spotlight on them. The best way to deal with them is to inform them that you are busy and politely suggest that they come back to chat another time. As long as your tone and demeanour remain calm and friendly, the show-off will not be too chagrined by you. Remember that as the newcomer, the last thing you want to do is to alienate yourself from your co-workers, so be courteous to everyone in the office, even time-wasters.

The Territorial

For the territorial type, the workplace is a crucial part of life. Their office or cubicle is their universe, and the work that they do is their entire world. Territorial types are extremely protective of their work area and purview. They are not always keen to reach out and offer assistance to others. Their main concern is to keep their own territory intact and ensure that senior management recognizes their solitary efforts. They are also quick to point out other people's mistakes or flawed methods, especially if these make someone other than themselves look incompetent. To the rest of the team this approach can be frustrating, but in the territorial's mind, they are just playing fair. Territorial types do not make good team players. In order to keep the peace, just be aware of the territorial's point of view and respect their space.

The office environment is not entirely made up of unsavoury personalities. Most companies have a healthy balance of people with good and bad personalities represented in their offices. Employers cannot always tell an individual's personality at the time of hiring, even if they use psychometric personality testing. Potential hires are usually on their best behaviour when they start a new job and only default to their true nature when they are comfortably settled into their roles. Whether this is a good or bad thing is open for discussion, but my personal view is that offices are microcosms of the real world, and some co-workers are going to be easier to get along with than others, so you might as well get used to it. The positive aspect to this reality is that some people always make an effort to be pleasant, and their personalities at work remain consistent. An example of a congenial personality type that can be found in the office environment is the introvert. Those quiet types are quite possibly the smartest and most hardworking people around, and they like to let their work speak for itself. Introverts tend to be "doers" and don't fritter their time away in idle gossip or tittle-tattle, so it is a mistake to confuse introversion or quietness for ineptitude. Unless they are passive-aggressive towards you, which is an unattractive tactic used to intimidate, show them respect and focus on your own performance.

Summary

- Make your first impression count; you don't get a second chance to make another one.
- Make an effort to get to know your co-workers.
- Find ways to remember people's names and take the initiative in introducing yourself to those you haven't met.
- If you are uncertain about something, therein lies the perfect opportunity to strike up a conversation with someone. Being new, you can get away with being a little forward and approach people who are probably above your level by asking an innocent question. However, do not overdo this lest you become a pest and people start avoiding you.
- Ask if you can tag along to lunch with one of the other secretaries soon after commencing your new position to get some pointers about the organization.
- Remember, the bully is not only in school but is in the workplace as well. Learning to shrug these undesirables off will put you in good stead.
- Always keep in mind that the most important person to you at your workplace is your boss.
- Ask your boss for feedback at the end of your first week and then at the end of your probationary period in order to gauge your progress and determine whether you are a "good fit" for him and for the company. This gives the two of you a chance to chat and further develop your relationship and rapport.
- Identify and be acquainted with the VIP in your organization and remember that they have the power to shape your future.
- Maintain professionalism in your work and interactions with others.
- Manage your time wisely.
- Use common sense in gauging urgent requests and the need to escalate them.

- Treat everyone around you with dignity and respect and this will carry you far in your career.
- Do not concern yourself with anyone else's performance. Focus solely on your own.
- Maintain an awareness of the personality types in your office and how to work well with them.

Be aware of a company's unwritten rules – these *are* the politics!

Chapter 5: Office Politics

Office Politics 101

Depending on your vantage point, you can look at office politics as a positive or a negative aspect of working life. Much like people who view the glass as half full rather than half empty, secretaries who understand that office politics are a fact of office life will make a smoother transition into an organization's culture. Unless you find yourself in a situation that you feel is completely untenable, office politics need not be viewed as daunting and threatening but rather as a challenge and opportunity to learn and grow.

The issue of politics is broad and its exact definition is difficult to pinpoint, so suffice it to say that it can be "sticky." The question is how you respond when you find yourself in the midst of a political situation. Secretaries who work in a highly politicized atmosphere must possess exceptional interpersonal skills in order to adjust to their new environment.

At any level in an organization, people behave as all career-conscious professionals do. They form alliances, and certain people are in cahoots with others in order to protect or advance their careers. This isn't necessarily a bad thing – it is just politics. As a secretary, you must be aware of what personality types you find most difficult to work with, and you must have an action plan to strategically place yourself in the political setting involved and manage to somehow fit in. (See "Unsavoury Personality Types" in chapter 4 of this book.)

I can remember a time in my career when I supported two individuals who were a study in opposites. One of the managers (I'll refer to him as Mr. Day) had hired me and was superb to work for, while I struggled with the other (Mr. Night), because he was always uncongenial and frosty no matter how much I smiled or went above and beyond to please him. Mr. Night would never look me in the eye when addressing me. His eyes would wander out the window, around my office, onto my computer, just about anywhere but directly at me. While Mr. Day and I engaged in office banter, Mr. Night did not and seemed to resent it. When I arrived for work each morning, I would make an effort to go and greet both bosses, and the responses to my greetings were always very different. Mr. Day would inquire with genuine interest about my weekends and engage in a dialogue with me, while Mr. Night would exchange the obligatory pleasantries with me or look up at the clock immediately upon my entry into the office, which indicated that he was "clocking" me every morning. Sometimes I would greet Mr. Night and he would reply without even looking up from his computer, as if my saying hello was an unnecessary interruption.

The political dimension in this environment was the fact that I really liked Mr. Day, whom I got along with well, but for obvious reasons I didn't much like Mr. Night. I also liked the company and was not inclined to quit my position as a result of a personality conflict with one manager. Like it or not, I had to figure out a way to work with both individuals. As an added complication, the two managers worked very closely together and got along really well. I realized that I could never approach one manager about the other, even if I was assured that the discussion was in the strictest of confidence. I understood office politics well enough not to do that. *This is office politics!*

When confronted with a similar situation, there really is no option but to figure out a way to make your new home work for you. You simply cannot run from office politics. If you do, I can *promise* you that office politics of a different kind will be waiting for you at your next job. They may be dressed up differently, but I have yet to hear of or encounter an office environment devoid of politics. However, if the politics within your organization clash with your personal values or you find that you simply cannot abide by them, then a graceful exit may be in good order.

Understanding Office Politics

Office politics are a fixture of office life. Secretaries are quite often affected by office politics and yet, at times, are oblivious to their existence. As a tenured secretary or one that is in a new position, you will quickly develop strategies for coping with office politics, and the true test will be how you respond to some of the sticky situations you find yourself in. Although trite at times, office politics should be taken seriously or at least acknowledged.

Office politics differ from organization to organization, and what works in one company may not necessarily be valid in another. The office politics playing out in small organizations can be just as complex as those in larger ones. In my experience, office politics tend to be magnified in confined spaces, be it a small office, small department, or small company. Since there are not many people in the office, any minor mode of conduct or action is keenly observed and analyzed. Employees in smaller offices also tend to form cliques, making it extremely difficult for one person to join the firm and integrate into it without causing ripples in the pre-existing office culture. However, smaller firms may be favourable to some, particularly non-profit organizations, because they can provide a level of flexibility that is often nonexistent in larger organizations.

In my experience, larger organizations are notoriously bureaucratic. This isn't to say that small firms do not have some level of bureaucracy, but the medium- to large-sized companies that I have worked in tended to be perpetually mired in bureaucracy. To get things done, there are processes and procedures to be followed and a chain of command to observe. The act of "pulling rank" is quite prevalent in larger organizations and is often integral to the politics. There were many times in my career when people "pulled rank" on me and it was very unpleasant. What do I mean by this? Staff pull rank when they assume that the secretary will handle certain jobs because she is at the lowest level of authority on the totem pole. Sometimes the secretary is even assigned roles without consultation. When this happens, a politically savvy secretary will temper her response to any situation that she deems unfair according to the politics at that organization.

Larger organizations can be preferable to some secretaries because they often implement policies that promote professionalism and address conduct in the workplace, which can be lacking in smaller firms. Typically, in larger organizations consisting of multilayered, hierarchical organizational structures, the conduct of employees is self-serving and driven by a strong desire for power, influence, recognition, or self-preservation. Indeed, one cannot fault this behaviour, because it denotes ambition, and there is nothing wrong with a healthy dose of ambition. Because of these differences, depending on your preference as a secretary, it can be difficult to adjust to working for a larger organization from a smaller firm, and vice versa.

There is some ambiguity in the public domain about the characterization and definition of a small business or company. This is likely because business classifications vary from country to country. In Canada, the government classifies the size of a business based on the number of employees in the organization:

- Small business—50 employees or fewer
- Medium-sized business—50 to 100 employees
- Large business—100+ employees

While the Government of Canada uses these classifications, the definitions in other countries will be different. According to the US Small Business Administration,[7] in that country the classification for a small business is 500 employees for manufacturing and mining industries and 100 employees for wholesale trade industries. In Europe, classifications vary yet again. It is little wonder then that when I

7 "US Small Business Administration, FAQs: Frequently Asked Questions, Size Standards," *SBA.gov*, accessed April 26, 2010, http://web.sba.gov/faqs/faqindex.cfm?areaID=15.

surveyed a group of secretaries about their interpretation of business size classifications, their perceptions were incongruent and varied. Some secretaries identified their companies as large firms because they had 100 employees but changed their minds when I asked them how they would classify an organization with 20,000 employees. Others viewed their firms of 100 employees as medium-sized entities. Suffice it to say that most secretaries view company size from the perspective of how many people they are required to support in proportion to the entire organization. As secretaries amass experience and are tenured in different-sized organizations, they begin to have a preference for firms of a certain size, derived in large part by their appetite for the specific political environment that firm tends to have.

The politics a secretary encounters in one organization can differ greatly from those she will find in another, because politics are driven by the existing structure (chain of command) of an organization and its particular culture (values, attitudes, and people). Each organization operates within its own hierarchy and dynamics. For example, if the culture at a particular firm dictates that anyone who is not at management level cannot join or utilize the on-site executive gym and spa, then all staff members below this status will likely see themselves as second-class citizens of that firm. In order to attain management status, some employees will play the political games that are necessary to gain the recognition they seek or need to be contenders.

The absence of rules surrounding office decorum can affect morale. Working in a small office at one stage in my career, I simply couldn't believe that my employer was prepared to tolerate the staff running amok in his office, yet he was. There were those who persistently sought attention by walking up and down the office corridors speaking in high-pitched voices at every opportunity, causing a disturbance for the more industrious employees. In other instances, some employees engaged in long lunch breaks or smoking breaks, often with a senior member of staff, which of course caused some discourse among those employees who diligently followed the rules and were not in cahoots with any senior staff. But again, office politics dictated that one couldn't really say or do anything about it because a senior staff member was participating in this unacceptable behaviour.

Office politics take many forms. The predominant kind has to do with hierarchy. As a seasoned secretary, experience teaches you that a president (CEO) garners enormous respect and gets superior service to that of his vice presidents, directors, and managers. Presidents will generally have a sprawling office with all the modern conveniences. They may get extras like a reserved parking space, a company vehicle, and the latest gadgets, while these may not be extended to the directors or managers, depending on company policy. Similarly, the vice president and/or company directors may enjoy many more perks than do their subordinates. When favouritism and certain privileges are extended to those who don't fit into the normal hierarchy for that company, you have a political situation. Other staff members who observe this favouritism will become incensed, but they will not speak up to the boss or anyone close to him for fear of reprisals.

Newcomers (secretaries in particular) joining any company have to study the hierarchy and educate themselves on the politics at play. When office politics turn nasty or if you find yourself embroiled in them, you need the right tools and political know-how to disentangle yourself with your reputation and professionalism intact.

Definitions of Office Politics

There is no single definition of office politics. A situation that a secretary considers political may appear perfectly normal to others. Here are seven definitions of office politics and how to respond to each situation.

1. A situation in which you, the secretary, quietly observe unprofessional conduct but cannot say or do anything about it on account of politics.

   A number of secretaries support bosses who travel a great deal or who are rarely in the office. If you are in that position, during the boss's absence you might observe your co-workers behaving in an unbecoming and unprofessional manner. For example, you might observe that certain people spend hours making personal phone calls when the boss is away, something they never do when he is present. You might also witness that others waste an enormous amount of the time they are paid to work in idle gossip when the boss is not in the office but reverse this behaviour in his presence. Even if this behaviour is deceitful and gives you the impression that some co-workers are not performing their jobs as they should, tread carefully. Speaking up or reporting this behaviour would not be good politics on your part because it will negatively affect your relationship with both your colleagues and your boss. While your boss might appreciate the information, he might also wish that you hadn't said anything because such accusations put him in a difficult position. On top of that, if a co-worker is lectured or disciplined as a result of your report, she will regard you as a traitor. Even if she was doing something wrong, she certainly won't thank you for the correction; indeed, it's likely she will never trust you again. This will make it difficult for you to work with her and her allies in the future, and her distrust and dislike of you may spread to others. If everyone in the office thinks you are acting as a spy for the boss, you will find yourself in an isolated position, which is dangerous if you need someone to back you up. As a secretary, I have observed this kind of political situation play out many times over, and as difficult as it is for the hardworking secretary to simply observe and not act upon such behaviour, that is what you must do.

2. A situation in the office environment that makes you or other staff members uncomfortable.

   An example of this definition is nepotism – a situation in which a relative of someone in power gets away with doing things that an ordinary employee would be disciplined for. For instance, a niece of the CEO works for the firm and is allowed to behave in a disagreeable manner, persistently coming into work late and taking long lunches. Her peers are forced to quietly endure and tolerate this behaviour because of her relationship with the CEO.

When nepotism is an accepted practice in an organization, it places a heavy burden on the other employees, particularly if the nepotism is fostered by someone with a great deal of influence in the firm. When newcomers don't take the time to acquaint themselves with the key players and educate themselves about "who's who" in the organization, they can place their own positions in jeopardy by doing or saying something that is viewed as politically incorrect, even if the division of labour appears to be uneven.

3. A situation where a manager appears to favour one or more employees over others.

   This arises when the boss favours someone in the office, for whatever reason, and it is tolerated because no one wishes to antagonize the manager. As a secretary, you will get the opportunity to observe this behaviour from a front-row seat. Unfair and inequitable as this may seem, it is the manager's prerogative, and professionalism dictates that the secretary simply blames it on office politics. One thing you absolutely cannot do is to betray your boss's trust by talking to co-workers about anything that, in your view, is a blemish on his character.

4. A certain way of doing things that is unique to a particular organization.

   It might be a tradition at a particular firm that everyone meets up once a month at the local pub for drinks, or to celebrate office birthdays. If you are a newcomer who chooses not to attend these social events, particularly in a small firm, you may be viewed as antisocial, and your absence may give your co-workers the impression that you are not a team player. Office politics dictate that most people in the firm religiously attend these events not because they necessarily want to but because it is good politics to do so. Of course, if the environment is rife with favouritism or nepotism, the mere fact that others can get away with never having to attend these events while those employees with lesser influence have no alternative is another example of office politics.

5. Observance of and adherence to a strict hierarchy within an organization that isn't necessarily common business practice in others.

   This is very common in small firms or departments within larger organizations. In some companies, all decisions, big or small, will follow a strict procedure as to how they are handled or processed. For instance, it might be common practice that every single invoice or cheque crosses the CEO's desk. Some workers might regard this as overkill, but if this is the way it is done in this particular firm, office politics dictate that you just accept it as standard practice.

6. An accepted practice within an organization that is unique to that organization which would more than likely be frowned upon or met with disapproval in others.

   I believed that I had seen it all in my career, until I worked in an organization where people arbitrarily used the company's credit cards to make personal purchases. Even more disturbing was the fact that there was plenty of nepotism in the company, so much so that you couldn't go to your supervisor to voice your suspicions because the supervisor might be closely related to the offender. If you are a secretary who understands office politics, you will also be aware that the questionable behaviour of those in positions of power is just the way it is in some companies, and you must simply turn a blind eye. If the conduct of certain employees goes unchallenged by senior management, then right or wrong, it is considered acceptable.

7. A situation in which someone with influence reneges or goes back on their word to placate others in the interest of politics.

   Things happen in organizations that might seem unfair to a secretary. For example, say a secretary is fired or a vacancy goes unfilled, and this doubles your workload. Your boss may promise to rectify the situation by ensuring that the resource void is addressed, either by hiring on someone else or passing the task to another individual in the firm. However, due to whatever politics at the organization, whether budget or resourcing constraints, your boss reneges and states that you simply have to accept the situation in the interim or long term. The boss may be playing politics, but sometimes he has to; similarly, if you like your job and the company, you cannot take this personally – you too must play politics and accept the additional task. Get used to it – it is just office politics!

Fighting for Power and Prestige

The dirtiest word in the corporate world is "power." Although one would be hard-pressed to obtain an admission of guilt in this regard, nearly everyone in a high-net-worth organization is jostling for some kind of eminence over his or her peers. Power and prestige are highly coveted.

Along with the power struggles one encounters in the office environment is the ever-present fight for prestige in the form of an office with a window. The question of who gets which office can present a set of challenges for the employer and employees alike – often contentious ones. This political issue varies in its extremity based on the unique organizational structure and culture involved. There are a great number of companies that afford senior secretaries an office, and it's no big deal. However, in companies where such an act is a novelty, the introduction of such a policy can become a prickly political issue, particularly for the excluded parties.

Office space is at a premium in most big cities, and as such the modern offices of the twenty-first century have morphed into open-plan, cubicle-inhabited work areas. To counter office politics, employers need to have policies in place that every employee understands.

As a secretary, you can be exposed to simultaneously cantankerous and amusing behaviour from senior managers that might be driven by a struggle for power or a need to self-promote. More often than not, you will find yourself feeling unimportant and slightly inadequate, especially during those times when a certain contingent among the managers, directors, or vice presidents are clamouring for recognition or pursuing their own personal agendas.

The constant gripe from the majority of secretaries interviewed for this book was that a certain contingent of the so-called corporate VIPs is disrespectful to the profession. From the secretary's perspective, far too often there is a tendency to pay little attention to her unless and until the individual is looking for a favour, or to use the secretary in some professional capacity (for filing, help with a project, travel assistance, or running errands). They further stated that some managers tend to be condescending to anyone who does administrative work, because they assume that a secretary's intelligence is limited to the administrative functions of her job. I must stress that while this type of behaviour comes with the territory and bears mention, not all managers or senior management share this frame of mind.

I have encountered many secretaries afflicted with a serious inferiority complex, and in order to attain some semblance of power within their organization, they use their boss's position and title to leverage some authority within the firm, imposing this on people they believe to be beneath them in rank. Such behaviour may be unconscionable, but it is usually a reflection of their low self-esteem.

Within the corporate world, situations and people may not always appear as they seem. Some people become quite obsessive about their personal agendas – a big motivator of their behaviour towards you, or their targeted "meal ticket." Secretaries must be aware of this yet remain professional despite undesirable behaviour among such so-called professionals.

In any given organization, the president's secretary has significant influence among the secretarial crowd and management simply because she has the ear of the president, is privy to a lot of confidential information, and is a trusted confidante to her boss. Usually, she is referred to as the senior executive secretary by virtue of whom she reports to. While her role may be no different from yours, to play the office politics game is to accept these established practices and treat her with the respect she feels is her due.

Some years ago I joined a commercial property management firm in London, England, where I broke some office politics rules and later lived to regret it. I was working for a director in the firm, and I failed to realize that one particular secretary worked for someone higher up on the totem pole than my boss. Office politics dictated that she was superior to me in rank. But I refused to recognize her higher rank – in my eyes she was my equal, and no more intelligent than I was – and by being non-compliant and disrespectful of the chain of command, I was labelled as a belligerent non-team player. I suffered for my folly and learned the hard way to simply go along with the politics. It makes life a lot easier. A seasoned secretary understands that such behaviour is part and parcel of the corporate world.

It is important to be adaptable in this line of work, and if you have aspirations to work for the head of a company or anyone at the executive level, you must be aware that his outgoing assistant will have a lot to say about who is hired as a replacement. If you really want to climb the secretarial ladder, you need to be mindful that secretaries working at the executive level supporting a president, CEO, or vice president do carry some clout, and they can influence your career within that organization. More generally, office politics dictate that such practices are what they are. They are not written anywhere. They just exist, and that's all there is to it. To question them would be tantamount to meddling with the status quo, and one does this at one's peril.

Political Games

An astute secretary ensures that she is continually well versed in the political nuances of her particular organization and always aware of its chain of command. For instance, if a customer complaint came in for a particular department, she would probably adhere to the unstated rules of office politics and proceed to direct the issue or complaint to the correct individual, making sure not to bypass him or her or handle the complaint herself, as doing so would create a bad situation all around.

Politics are as much about the culture in the organization as they are about the organization itself. Management sets the tone for organizational politics, and the employees respond in a manner that placates management while serving their individual interests. In my view, management is as responsible for the political climate in an organization as the people who work there. When senior management allows certain behaviour from their staff, they are endorsing the office politics that occur under their watch. If staff members frequently engage in office tittle-tattle, and rather than discouraging it, managers join in, the staff members who are victims of this type of behaviour are rendered powerless to adequately respond to gossip-mongering or similar behaviour in their work environment.

When corporate policies are put in place for guiding professional conduct in an organization and the employer does not enforce those policies or there appears to be a double standard, negative outcomes are inevitable. Some employees will take advantage of this lack of leadership, while others will resent it. The resulting incongruity translates into a political climate that is viewed positively by some and negatively by others.

One secretary I interviewed – for the purposes of this book I will call her Anne – was very bitter about her previous position. She believed that she was the "sacrificial lamb" sent to slaughter for the sake of keeping the peace. Anne was a secretary in the acquisitions department of a property development firm in the United Kingdom. She worked for two directors, and her job consisted of a lot of audio transcription. The one director whom she worked for – we will call him Jack – was apparently never clear on his dictation. He chewed his words and spoke so softly that it was a mammoth task for Anne to complete his transcription work. Anne had told Jack on many occasions that his tapes were taking longer and longer to complete because of the quality of his dictation. Jack took offence at being addressed in this manner by a secretary and decided to show her who was boss by making her work life even more difficult.

Anne decided to appeal to the other director she assisted – we will call him Mike. What Anne failed to realize was that the two directors were drinking buddies, so her appeal fell on deaf ears. Anne grew more and more frustrated. Meanwhile, Jack refused to change his dictation technique but instead started taking copies of Anne's work, noting the number of errors in her transcriptions, and surreptitiously showing them to the department head. In no time, the department head called Anne into his office and told her she was being let go for poor performance.

Anne appealed her case, but it was no use because she had no one to back her up. Unbeknownst to her, in order to support each other, both Mike and Jack had complained about the quality of her work to the department head! They wanted her gone so they could hire a new secretary and have a say about who would assist the two of them rather than dealing with an inherited secretary, as Anne was. No matter which way you look at it, this was a case of pure office politics. Anne may have had grounds for unfair dismissal, but even she knew that it was a futile exercise to pursue legal action; she would never win, had nothing to back up her story, and hadn't been smart enough to keep some of the dictation tapes to present to the department head to explain her frustration.

If Anne had understood the rules of office politics within her work environment, she could have adjusted the way she handled this issue to ensure that she did not rock the boat. One way Anne could have handled this situation differently would have been to approach Jack right from the outset in a non-confrontational manner and explain that she was having difficulty understanding him on tape and astutely offer an alternative, such as asking for handwritten notes or taking the dictation by hand herself as opposed to getting it on tape. Approaching him the way that she did may have antagonized and infuriated him. Here was his secretary highlighting his weaknesses, so he may have decided right then and there to teach her a lesson. If Anne had known how to play the office politics game, her approach might have been different and she might not have lost her job.

With respect to your immediate boss, never assume that things will not get back to him. It only takes one person who dislikes your attitude or professional conduct to drive a wedge between you and your boss that could jeopardize your position. Treat everyone equally and with respect because you never know who your boss might be tomorrow!

More often than not, when you join a new company, the group of secretaries in that organization will have already established alliances. There may be little cliques of two, three, or four. Be careful not to be drawn into these alliances whose mandate you know nothing about. Remember who hired you, and if that person is happy to have you on the team, that is all that matters. It is good to be a team player, but you have to be mature enough to know when to draw the line, and if the conversation turns to gossip-mongering, take that cue to excuse yourself. In my book, gossip-mongering is a sign of immaturity, jealousy, and low self-esteem. Rise above it and excuse yourself when the talk gets dirty!

Do not always assume that your boss will back you up or defend you in a political fracas because he or she may choose to placate the other party and leave you high and dry. Sometimes your immediate boss may engage in politics that benefit him but discredit and dishonour your personal integrity and trust. When this occurs, it is very difficult to get over the disappointment that your boss sold you out. What should you do if this situation arises? It depends on a number of things. If you love your job and like your boss, you may choose to write his behaviour off to office politics. But for many, this is easier said than done. Office politics can help define your true relationship with your boss. When politics are at play, will he support you, or as the saying goes in North America, will he "throw you under the bus'? It can be quite a challenge to not take office politics personally, but this is what you must not do.

The Holiday Party

A highly politicized situation to watch for is the office holiday party. This is something that may appear on the surface as a no-holds-barred, anything-goes type of event, but it isn't. In fact, it's anything but. Having been to as many as fourteen of these shindigs, I have learned a thing or two. The presumption on your part may be that you can relax, have a good time, dare to pinch your boss's bottom, and pluck up the courage to land an uninvited kiss on that cute guy from the advertising department. *Wrong*! You will pay for your unruly behaviour because everyone will dissect the events on the day after, and while it may seem to you that everyone had a little too much to drink, remember that appearances can be deceiving. I have heard people labelled by many names the day after a holiday party; these labels generally weren't very nice and can be real career-breakers.

I recall an incident I witnessed when a secretary got absolutely intoxicated and approached her boss, who had been drinking nothing but lemonade all night. She tried to commandeer him onto the dance floor with her in slurry, drunken speech, and right away he turned on his heel without a word and went across the room to speak to another senior executive. A group of us simultaneously dropped our jaws in shock as we witnessed the unfolding drama. The secretary in question suddenly called her boss by his first name. "Don't walk away from me when I'm talking to you!" she shouted. "I command you to come and dance with me now, or I will keep following you around the room!" At this juncture, although the music was quite loud, a number of people were witnessing this debacle in horror. Undeterred, the secretary then started towards the other side of the room, following her boss while shouting his name. With her glass in hand, she missed her step and went crashing to the floor.

Her boss moved even farther towards the end of the room in complete embarrassment; meanwhile, someone assisted the drunken girl and escorted her out of the party.

Needless to say, the drunken secretary was the talk of the after-party. Relations between the executive and this secretary were further strained. Following a few other incidents, the secretary quit her position, citing a communication breakdown between her and her boss. That whole incident and the issues arising from it was another political situation. As a secretary, you do not want to get yourself entangled in those kinds of situations, because they will earn you notoriety. Furthermore, you cut yourself off from possible promotions and ruin your chances for a bright and successful career. Remember, you rely on your boss to give you a reference for your next position, and the lack of a glowing reference may stand between you and that next dream job. A seasoned and well-trained secretary who understands corporate politics knows and adheres to the boundaries of acceptable behaviour at any given event, especially a holiday party.

While on the topic of holidays and bosses, most good bosses will treat their secretaries to a wonderful gift each year. It isn't necessary for the secretary to reciprocate; her boss does not expect anything in return. In fact, many have confessed that a secretary's reciprocal gift creates awkwardness in the relationship. If you are one of the lucky secretaries working for a considerate boss who showers you with beautiful gifts, all you need to do is say "Thank you" – your boss doesn't expect and quite possibly doesn't want you to buy him something in return.

Unwanted Romantic Advances

It is possible that your superior will extend the boundaries of your relationship by flirting or suggesting the two of you see each other outside the office in a romantic setting. The manner in which you reject the advances is the key to handling this situation. If you make a big deal about it or try to belittle your boss, he won't like it. The shame and embarrassment that he will feel will backfire on you, and you will indeed jeopardize your career. My advice is to reject any such advances politely and in a respectful manner. Furthermore, as soon as the moment has passed, do not dwell on the matter, conduct yourself as though nothing untoward happened. Do not dwell on the matter.

Summary

- Study your company's hierarchy and follow established practices.
- Be aware of a company's unwritten rules – these *are* the politics.
- Avoid succumbing to pre-established alliances – being pleasant and professional will suffice.
- Your number one priority in the organization is and always will be your boss's needs, and your first loyalty is to him and those higher up in the chain of command.
- Avoid making unqualified assumptions; they could cost you your job. Seek advice instead.
- Own up to situations you don't know or understand rather than pretending to be in the know. Such pretence is foolish and may backfire.
- Maintain your integrity and decorum at all official company events, particularly the holiday parties.
- There is no need to buy your boss a gift in reciprocation.

Chapter 6:
The Job

What is a secretary, after all? The raw truth of the matter is that a secretary is an assistant to someone of a higher rank or level within any organization, be it a small or large firm, private practice or establishment. Secretaries can be found in as many varied positions as there are industries. The role of a secretary is primarily administrative in nature and never was intended to be a position of authority.

The word "secretary" contains the word "secret" within it, and this is no coincidence. The term itself is derived from the Latin words *secernere*, meaning "to set apart," and the word *secretarius*. Between the late-fourteenth century and the nineteenth century, a secretarius was a confidante to a king or pope, tasked with keeping records and writing letters. Up until the nineteenth century, men entrusted with keeping secrets for powerful individuals assumed the title of secretary. Today one thing still holds true: secretaries keep secrets for their bosses and sometimes for the organizations that employ them. Most secretaries run their boss's personal and professional lives and are entrusted with the most privileged information of a personal and business nature. Professional secretaries are expected to be extremely discreet and loyal to their employers, even in the absence of a non-disclosure and confidentiality agreement. A secretary who cannot be trusted to keep things to herself will not go far in this line of work.

Today, most managers and secretaries prefer the title "assistant" to that of "secretary," and although the label "assistant" is more apt, refusing the title "secretary" is futile and simply a matter of semantics because there is no difference in the function or role. The masses might agree to rename you "administrative assistant," "executive assistant," "personal assistant," or anything else you might choose, but they still consider you a secretary. It is similar to calling a telemarketer by some other obscure title when the functionality and general understanding of this profession remains unchanged in the mind of the public.

The *Oxford English Reference Dictionary* states that an assistant is the following:

1. a helper
2. a person who assists, esp. as a subordinate in a particular job or role

The same dictionary describes a secretary working in business or professional firms as "a person employed by an individual or in an office etc. to assist with correspondence, keep records, make appointments etc."

An assistant is an enabler, and if she is very good, her manager will come to rely heavily on her expertise and be completely lost without her. She anticipates his needs and knows everything about the running of his office. If she is truly exceptional, when her manager calls her into his office she walks in holding the file that he is about to request and hands it to him. She plans all his travel ahead of time, and these trips always run smoothly. In fact, her ability to keep things running smoothly at all times is visibly noticeable even when she must be absent from her job.

Each position a prospective secretary applies for will have a job description, and if it does not, it is up to the candidate to request one either at the interview or at the beginning of the assignment. Many secretaries tend to skim through job descriptions, then cry foul when they have accepted a position and realize that they actually have to run some errands for their boss or make coffee for his guests. Review the job description thoroughly, because for the next several years of your life, those tasks will be the backbone of your job.

Not too long ago in my own career, I made the mistake of not listening to my own advice and accepted a position on the basis of assumption. I assumed the position would bring me interesting and challenging work, and I assumed that I would be very busy given my new boss's title. I assumed many things that never came to pass. Other than a generalized job outline that was posted with the job advertisement, I wasn't given a proper job description and I did not request one either. The job itself was a huge disappointment on many levels. However, had I reviewed the job description or asked the right questions at the interview, I might have had a much better sense of what I was walking into.

The Reality of the Job

The true role of a secretary is to eliminate the mundane office tasks and daily minutiae from the manager's workflow, leaving the manager free to concentrate on the more important issues called for in his position. That is not to say that the secretary's role is inferior, unimportant, or mundane. On the contrary, secretaries are the cornerstone of many an organization. Highly proficient and experienced secretaries are real masters at what they do, and such individuals are rare. They are skilled in all aspects of running an office and multitasking, from their mastery of external relations when representing the company they work for to being excellent negotiators, and in some cases they are known to be very good communicators. For instance, they are required (sometimes daily) to negotiate with travel agents, hotels, event planners, and restaurants and must get past mammoth gatekeepers to set up meetings for higher-echelon executives in other organizations as well as managing complex schedules and other administrative tasks.

The work done by secretaries has long been misunderstood. Gone are the days when secretaries simply answered the telephone, typed the odd letter, and made coffee. Consider the way secretaries are depicted in the AMC television show *Mad Men*. Although the show accurately captures the confines of the role in the 1960s, it is those misconceptions, old-school attitudes, and mystique looming over the new generation of secretaries that spurred me to write this book. Secretaries in the new computer age are multi-skilled and multitalented. They work in comfortable surroundings (upscale, for a lucky few), using the most advanced technology of the times. Besides the well-known administrative component of their job function and the evermore discretionary nature of the work that they are exposed to, the more senior secretaries of today enjoy a multifaceted portfolio that may include the following key responsibilities:

- research and data analysis
- complex national and international travel planning coordination
- management of the boss's personal matters such as banking and running errands
- basic accounting
- credit card and expense reconciliation
- development of communication procedures
- execution of special projects
- coordination of board packages and logistics for board meetings
- drafting correspondence and acting as a delegate for the boss at meetings and events

Secretaries are well versed in all technical and administrative trends in the market, especially those that impact the industry that they represent. As new desktop gadgets, computer programs, and software come onto the market, bosses rely on their secretaries to test drive the product or service to determine the usefulness for their organization. The advent of personal computers, the BlackBerry®, the iPad®, the iPhone®, and other mobile devices may aid an executive in performing some of his own tasks. He can use portable communication devices (PCDs) to bypass his secretary by sending his own e-mails and text messages. However, he still needs his secretary to follow up on some e-mails, phone calls, and "past due" action items. The secretary will also type many of the attachments that may be required to accompany e-mails, checking the spelling and grammar on all his written output.

10 Rules for the Elite Secretary

Irrespective of where you are on your secretarial journey, here are my top 10 recommended rules of conduct. These rules form the key requirements for an elite secretary:

1. *Be Ethical*

Do what is right all of the time. Engage in ethical behaviour by treating everyone you encounter with dignity and fairness.

2. *Live with Integrity*

Having integrity means abiding by a code of moral values, and determining how you behave and conduct yourself even when nobody is looking. Accordingly, conduct yourself with the utmost integrity in all that you do.

3. *Be Honest*

Honesty and integrity go hand in hand. An honest person has integrity, and vice versa. Be honest all the time regardless of the circumstances, though this trait must be balanced by both discretion and tact in a secretary.

4. *Be Respectful*

Treat *everyone* you encounter as you like to be treated. Be cognizant that the respect you show others may not be reciprocated; be respectful nonetheless.

5. *Be Efficient*

Raise the bar for the profession, and do your best to complete assigned tasks efficiently. To be an *inefficient* secretary is an oxymoron.

6. *Be Professional*

The word "professional" has been thrown around a great deal, and its meaning has become diluted.

The label "professional" implies that one is an expert in his or her field. For secretaries, professionalism means being educated, competent, experienced, businesslike, and efficient. It is the opposite of being an amateur. Govern yourself accordingly if you call yourself a professional secretary.

7. *Be Discreet*

Remember, the "secret" in secretary means discretion is always required.

8. *Be Reliable*

Secretaries are secret-keepers for and confidantes of their bosses. This is impossible to achieve if you are unreliable.

9. *Be Punctual*

Part of the role of the secretary is to manage her boss's schedule. To show your organizational skills, strive to be punctual always.

10. *Communicate Effectively*

Remember that speaking and listening are twin skills in communication. Be both truthful and courteous in all your communications.

Competency Framework

In an effort to align their strategic goals with superior performance, forward-looking organizations establish competency management systems for their key job positions.

A competency framework or model is a collection of skills, abilities, or attributes that spotlights talented performers in an organization while identifying and providing development opportunities for others. Competency frameworks are knowledge based and designed specifically with an organization's strategic goals and competitive advantage in mind. A typical competency framework will consist of core competencies that every employee must possess or be working towards.

For secretaries, the process presents an opportunity to self-assess their skills according to their employer's requirements. The competency profile for secretaries can be measured using whatever proficiency levels the organization deems necessary for the role. After the self-assessment, the secretary can take steps to manage her own career through professional development.

To be successful and compliant with the organization's core competencies, the secretary must demonstrate that she is aware of the requirements of her role. Further, she must undertake the necessary training to advance to the next level of expertise.

Figure 7 - Key Competencies for the Elite Secretary

KEY COMPETENCIES	DESCRIPTION
Time management	The ability to use your time wisely and effectively during the core working hours is essential for success • Maintaining a disciplined approach to prioritizing and executing tasks • Timely and efficient execution of deliverables • Systematic planning and structure around your own work processes • Establishing priorities and anticipating future needs • Monitoring and regularly evaluating ongoing projects • Committing oneself to continuous improvement

Organizational skills	The capability to introduce, institute, and streamline processes and procedures that aid in the smooth and efficient running of the office • Demonstrating exceptional organization and multitasking abilities in document control and records management • Following a systematic and efficient method of performing tasks • Committing oneself to continuous process improvement
Communication skills	Possessing exceptional verbal, written, and listening skills in individual and group situations • Having the ability to communicate with all levels of management • Maintaining a strong internal and external network • Paying keen attention to detail • Being able to organize and present ideas in a meaningful, grammatically correct form
Interpersonal relations	Demonstrating an understanding of the feelings and needs of others • Exhibiting the capacity for warmth and tolerance • Being outgoing and sociable • Showing interest in seeking out and developing relationships with others
Discretion	Having the ability to perform tasks requiring a high degree of job sensitivity and confidentiality • Trustworthy • Honest • Possessing integrity

Initiative	Taking personal responsibility and ownership for meeting objectives • Setting challenging goals or high standards for personal achievement • Maintaining focus on the status and progress of personal goals and objectives
Technical skills	Proficiency in using a personal computer • Excellent computer navigation and keyboarding skills • Advanced knowledge of Microsoft Office
Level-headed	Maintaining effective performance in uncertain or unstructured situations, or when there is unusual pressure • Displaying a calm demeanour in stressful situations
Team player/teamwork	Demonstrating interpersonal communications with a wide range of individuals and personality types • Maintaining a positive attitude • Promoting a positive atmosphere in the workplace • Being open to working with a variety of people
Problem solving	Taking a proactive approach to troubleshooting • Adopting a proactive role in recognizing deficiencies • Identifying and creating efficiencies

Male Secretaries

You might be wondering where male secretaries fit in in this profession. Secretarial work is still saddled with the impression that women should fill the roles. They have their own niche but are still a minority group in the corporate world. Personally, I have encountered very few male secretaries in the course of my career, but I believe that as the times continue to change, male secretaries will become the norm and be accepted, just as male nurses and nannies are today. There is real irony in this modern stereotype, since men dominated the profession in the seventeenth century as "typists" and stenographers.[8] Today, even though they do exist, they are still vastly outnumbered by women, although accurate statistics on the number of male secretaries in the modern workforce are hard to come by. According to the 1996 census by Statistics Canada, the most common job for women five years prior was that of secretary.

It goes on to say, "The large decline in the number of secretaries reported in 1996 moved this occupation to second place."[9] The fact that the profession was reported as being the most common job for women in 1991 isn't surprising, nor is its drop to second place in the mid-nineties. As the new century approached, job opportunities for women were starting to open up in many other areas, which may explain the drop to second place in 1996.

A prominent male secretary of his time was John Doughty, who worked for the Toronto theatrical entrepreneur Ambrose J. Small from the early 1900s right up until the mysterious disappearance of the theatre magnate in 1919.[10] That same period was a defining period for female office workers, particularly in New York City, because a kind of role reversal took place. Women were hired in very large numbers to do office work, despite the fact that this had previously been viewed as strictly male territory. Today, the reverse is true; these jobs are very much viewed as female territory, with the occasional male considered an oddity in the profession.

---

8 Marjorie Gottlieb Wolfe Syosset, "Year-By-Year Chronology of the Secretarial Profession," accessed April 3, 2007, http://www.crazycolour.com/os/secretary_01.shtml.

9 Statistics Canada, *The Daily*, March 17, 1998, accessed May 24, 2005, http://www.statcan.gc.ca/daily-quotidien/980317/dq980317-eng.htm.

10 "The Disappearance of Ambrose Small – Case Closed," *Russianbooks.org*, accessed October 16, 2005, http://www.russianbooks.org/small.htm.

There are many forums and message boards on the Internet where discussion is ongoing about the small number of male secretaries in the workplace. However, the male secretaries who share their experiences on the Internet do so sparingly. I read a very interesting account of a male secretary's experience in the field. The article, which appeared in the *New York Times* in the 1980s, reinforced the fact that when men dared to join the secretarial field, they were viewed with suspicion. The secretary aptly described the significance of choosing the field: "I was bucking societal preconceptions. I was upsetting the established order. Or some such thing."[11] A particularly interesting perspective was posted by a former male secretary on a forum, giving an account of the highs and lows of his experience and confirming the notion that men in this profession are in the minority.[12] Other discussions concerning male secretaries paint a different and often unflattering picture of the role based on the experiences an individual has endured. One male assistant wrote a blog that he titled, "I am a male administrative assistant – and no, I'm not gay." He goes on to outline his work experiences and why and how he chose the profession, but it is his concluding remarks that I found most intriguing. "My one piece of advice for any future administrative assistants out there: interview your boss. If you don't get a good vibe from him or her, don't take the job." This is sage advice for every secretary.

If you are a young man finishing school and it is your dream to join the secretarial ranks, you should persevere unabated. Opportunities for male secretaries do exist, and some fields actually appear to favour them. For instance, there does seem to be a confluence of male assistants in

---

11 Joseph Finder, "About Men: A Male Secretary," *The New York Times*, February 22, 1987, www.nytimes.com/1987/02/22/magazine/about-men-a-male-secretary.htm.

12 "Male Administrative Assistant, and no, I'm not gay," *About My Job: Corporate America*, accessed March 4, 2007, http://aboutmyjob.com/main.php3?action=displayarticle&artid=2045.

the political world who primarily work for prominent political figures.[13] The former personal assistant/aide to President Barack Obama, Reggie Love, is male. However, he was a unique kind of assistant; according to Wikipedia, his title was "the special assistant and personal aide,"[14] which indicates that the role is vastly different from a traditional secretary. The *Christian Science Monitor* lauded the Obama administration's appointment of Jeremy Bernard in an opinion piece on their website titled "For gender equality we need more male secretaries, like Obama's Jeremy Bernard." He was the first man to fill the role of social secretary to the White House. Clearly the times are changing.[15] While conducting research for this book, I had occasion to discuss the role of a male executive assistant to a member of Parliament. Other than advising that his role is much more specialized than that of a general secretary, he was very guarded and wouldn't divulge much, which is typical for someone working in a sensitive role in government.

Today, male secretaries are also prevalent in the celebrity assistant role; however, the job is not typically secretarial but much more varied. The responsibilities can encompass many different tasks, including travel planning, personal shopping, conversing with the media, typing spreadsheets, and even baby sitting, dog walking, and picking up the celebrity's dry cleaning. Think about it: If you were the assistant to a pop star or a famous actor, what would your job description be? It certainly would not be like the role of an executive secretary to the CEO of a conglomerate or a Fortune 500 company. This is not to say that either of these roles is unimportant or that secretaries work any less, simply

13 "Male Order: Male Secretaries not unusual in the Labour Party," *Irish Times*, accessed February 15, 2007, http://www.irishtimes.com/newspaper/weekend/1998/0214/98021400260.html.

14 "Reggie Love," *Wikipedia*, accessed November 18, 2010, http://en.wikipedia.org/wiki/Reggie_Love.

15 Dominique Gomez, "For gender equality we need more male secretaries, like Obama's Jeremy Bernard," *Christian Science Monitor*, accessed June 25, 2011, http://www.csmonitor.com/Commentary/Opion/2011/0228/for-gender-equality-we-need-more-male-secretaries-like-obama-s-Jeremy-Bernard.

that there are many different types of secretaries or assistants filling various kinds of roles.

Super Secretaries

Secretaries are the uncrowned public relations managers of this millennium, tasked with ensuring daily efficiency in the output or perception of the company that they represent, from the smallest businesses to the largest companies and transnational conglomerates. Most understand how their professionalism affects the bottom line, particularly through their own conduct of day-to-day business activities, ranging from eloquence on the telephone to ensuring that important documents representing the company reach their destinations. Any secretary's misstep, error in judgement, misconduct, sloppy work, lack of professionalism, or show of inexperience will reflect on the whole organization.

To be a super secretary requires diplomacy, tact, and above all else unflappability because there are many trying situations that come with this profession and you need to be prepared for anything, particularly when it comes to fostering a good relationship with the boss. The worst position for a secretary to find herself in is to realize that she has no respect for the person she works for—the one who ultimately pays her salary. As soon as this occurs, a smart secretary starts looking for another job because you cannot work for someone you do not respect. However, before jumping ship you need to ensure that where you are going is not an even worse situation. Careful thought and planning is essential before making career moves.

Well-heeled and busy senior executives will be the first to acknowledge the importance of the secretaries in their lives. They cannot do without them and are often lost without their secretaries-cum-assistants telling them what to do or where to go. If an executive suddenly goes from having a super secretary to a real dunce, he soon begins to appreciate the rarity and value of the former. If secretaries were removed from the office there would be disorganization, chaos, and time mismanagement, and managers and senior executives alike would have the added responsibility of performing another job function inadequately. Ironically, it is the few bad secretaries whose inefficiencies highlight the crucial role the vast majority of efficient secretaries play in a company's smooth operational flow, success, and reputation.

In order for the executive to manage his time efficiently, it is the secretary who organizes his daily appointments, avoiding conflicts and double-booking. It is the secretary who ensures that wherever the executive or manager is rushing to, the travel is meticulously prearranged. This is of paramount importance, particularly if it is an overseas trip, because air and ground transportation, hotel arrangements, and trips to airports and appointments need to be carefully planned to avoid mishaps. The preparations that secretaries make behind the scenes translate into smooth transitions from one activity to the next for the executive.

As you read this, it will become evident that secretaries play a crucial role in the lives of their bosses and are privy to some of the hilarious mishaps and incidents, cover-ups, apologies, and near-disasters that they alone defuse on their employer's behalf. For example, a very experienced executive secretary enlightened me about a strategy she used to cover for her boss's persistent punctuality problem. Realizing that he was consistently late for appointments, she devised a plan to ensure that his tardiness was well camouflaged from important clientele. Before entering an appointment in her boss's calendar, she would allot an extra fifteen minutes prior to the scheduled event to give him extra time to get to the appointment as well as reminding herself to call ahead if he was late regardless. This is the kind of foresight only an astute and experienced secretary could come up with and is just one example of the numerous office routines, tasks, and processes that make the job of a secretary imperative and indispensable.

Autonomy

A secretary who is comfortable in her work environment can mold her position into whatever she pleases, adding more responsibilities to her portfolio or subtracting them by delegating them to a junior support person. Some bosses are so dependent on their secretaries that they are included in their travel plans, so that wherever the boss goes the secretary follows. As senior executives rely more and more on their secretaries, the secretary of the future will hold a higher level of education (diploma or bachelor's degree), with a focus on business administration or a related field, and as she begins to disdain the title "secretary" in preference for the more apt "administrative assistant" or "executive assistant," much more will be expected of her. Her role will be more challenging but all the more rewarding.

Secretaries lucky enough to be working with the right boss, within the right company, and with the right balance of challenging and fulfilling work can look forward to a long and enviable career. I have known secretaries to stay dedicated to their bosses for the duration of their careers, developing a long-standing friendship and becoming lifelong confidantes to them. Some bosses have claimed that they trust their secretary over and above their own friends and family because the relationship is built on professional respect. Indeed, one interview I attended left me feeling as though the exiting secretary's shoes could never be filled. The executive in this case told me how devastated he was to be losing "his right hand," describing their relationship as one of "close friends" and her efficiency as a trait that he was sure going to miss. I was nothing less than dumbfounded when he stated that her leaving was a deep, personal loss for him. It was obvious this executive was very attached to his secretary and that the transition to new staff would be difficult for him.

Several years ago, I was filled with pride when I read a magazine article where one executive talked about his assistant as someone who runs his office "efficiently and effectively. I couldn't get through my day without her."[16] Another executive referred to his assistant as "much

16 Diann Daniel, "Five Keys to Getting and Keeping a Great Executive Assistant," *CIO Magazine*, April 25, 2007, accessed September 9, 2010, http://www.cio.com/article/106103/Five_Keys_to_Getting_and_Keeping_a_GreatExecutive_Assistant?page=1&taxonomyId=3123.

more than just a support staff person." He went on to describe her as his "right hand, mentor, cheerleader, and an anchor when needed." It is wonderful relationships such as these that exemplify the true joy of being a secretary – being appreciated, respected, and valued as a fully contributing member of the team.

My best years in this profession were during the 1990s in London, England. I worked for some of the best male and female bosses possible, and they became the motivators for my extended secretarial career. The experience of working in a myriad of industries and job functions stood me in good stead and positioned me well for experience of a different kind in another country – Canada.

Hierarchy

In all my years of supporting senior executives, I observed that the higher up the executive was on the corporate ladder, the less stressful the position and the more autonomy was afforded to the secretary. Why? Primarily because senior executives rarely share an assistant, and if they do, it is a maximum of three executives to one assistant. They delegate a lot of their work to the VPs and directors, who in turn will get their assistants/secretaries to do the administrative part required and simply report back to the senior executive. Senior executive assistants tend to work independently with minimum supervision; they are skilled at juggling multiple projects while remaining effective. The executives at this level are usually conversant with the appropriate functional use of their secretaries.

There is very little room for error when working for a senior executive. Everything the secretary does must be done right – it is expected. A certain level of maturity is also expected. Hence some of these senior executive assistants who work for high net worth companies will have a junior administrative assistant working solely to support the executive assistant. A senior executive assistant has an assistant of her own so she can focus on the executive's needs and enhance the smooth running of his office.

Alternatively, a secretary working for an inexperienced manager or one who is obtuse may have a difficult time if he is lacking in perception. However, some experienced secretaries view this as a welcome challenge to train their executives in the merits of optimizing their secretarial resource.

At the senior level of management, a secretary will do no less work than her juniors or counterparts, but the pressure is not as intense as that faced by a secretary supporting anywhere from three to ten managers (or more) who each demand the same level of priority for their work as the next. At the junior level, a secretary may answer to so many people that in order to cope, she has to be extremely unflappable or she will flounder under the pressure. A position where a secretary's supporting role is split among a number of different managers can prove to be the best training for her. It prepares her for the demands of higher-profile positions at the senior management level.

The organizational chart in figure 8 shows a clear demarcation of the secretarial role and how it is directly linked to that of her immediate boss. The example represents a successful firm wherein each executive has his own secretary (or personal assistant), presumably because the executive's role warrants a dedicated secretary and the organization's pockets are deep enough for the extravagance. It is worth noting that on rare occasions, an executive will retain a secretary even if he doesn't really need one. He will typically do this for appearances' sake and to satisfy his "executive ego." The executive may not be able to keep that one secretary busy, but will continue to pay her salary for the privilege of having a secretary as a status symbol. Giving up his secretary would be tantamount to revealing the fact that he is not very busy, thereby putting his own position in jeopardy.

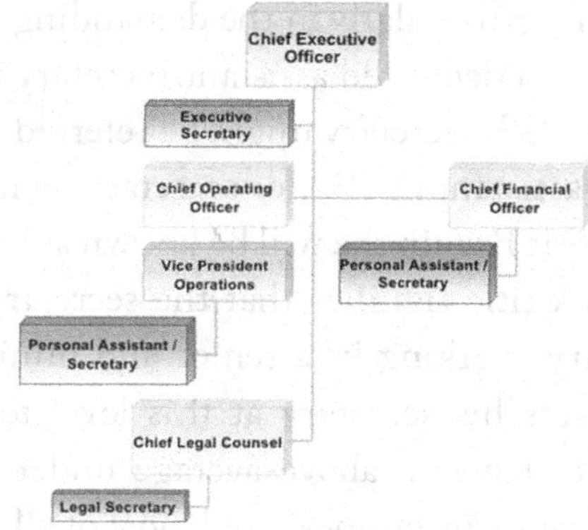

Figure 8 – Organizational Chart

In most instances, the CEO will have his own secretary. Her title in this case is usually either that of executive secretary or senior secretary. The perception exists that secretaries working at the most senior level of management have "cushy" jobs, and while in a majority of cases this is true, the job itself is still very challenging and all prior experience proves advantageous.

In smaller organizations and companies, the CEO, CFO, and COO might share one secretary between them (see figure 9). While the CEO will demand the lion's share of the secretary's time, the secretary will learn to fit the other two executives into her work schedule just as loyally. These obligations make for a very demanding and busy position. As a general assistant for three people, the secretary might also be referred to as the executive assistant.

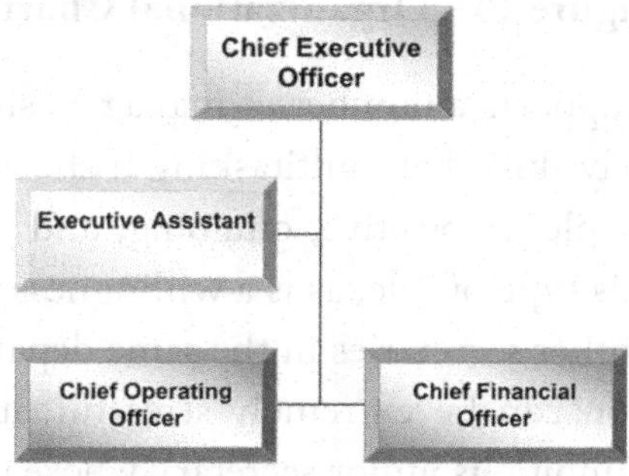

Figure 9 – Organizational Chart

A vice president (VP), particularly in the demanding field of sales, will most certainly require a dedicated assistant/secretary (see figure 10). In North America, the VP's secretary might be referred to as an executive assistant (EA), VP assistant (VPA), or secretary, while in Europe and most certainly in Great Britain she will be known as a personal assistant (PA). The PA or EA title signifies that the secretary is a level above an ordinary secretary, working in a senior and minimally supervised role. The boss expects his secretary at this level to be professional, to be dependable, to have an above-average understanding of office procedures and the company business, and most of all, to possess loyalty and discretion.

In larger organizations, two or three directors will share a secretary. The support level is even greater in some smaller companies with a limited budget, where it is quite possible that a secretary could work for three to five directors and/or managers.

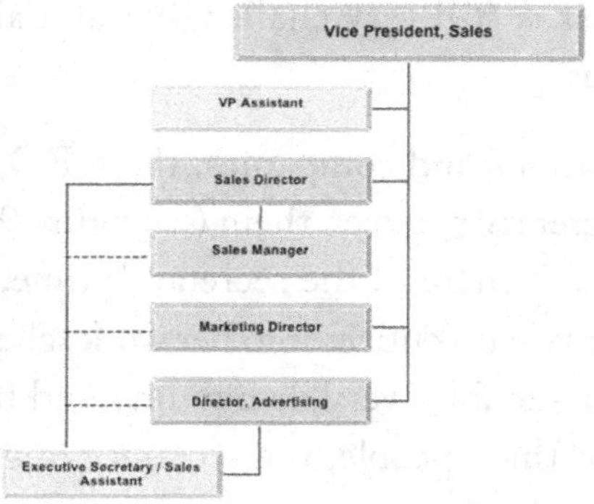

Figure 10 – Organizational Chart

When a secretary supports a number of managers simultaneously, she needs to be extremely skilled at multitasking if she is to cope with the demands of such a role. A positive, outgoing, and mature attitude is more suitable for this type of role, as is a willingness to equitably share the workload with other secretaries in the same department. Although this type of position can be extremely stressful, it can be the best preparation for an ambitious junior secretary whose ultimate goal is to work for a senior executive such as a very busy president or CEO.

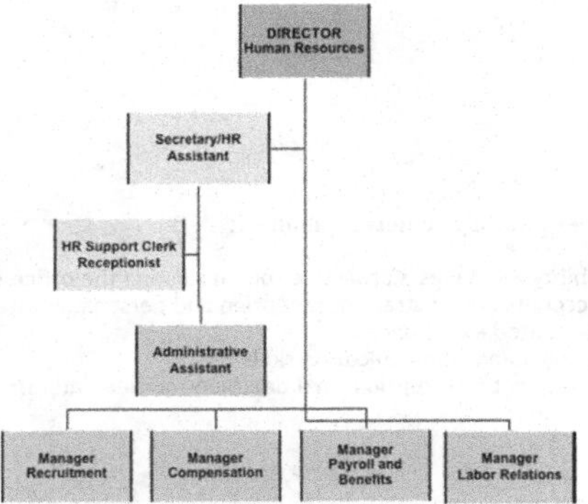

Figure 11 – Organizational Chart

Figure 11 illustrates most secretarial roles and the structures within which they operate. A busy executive such as a director of human resources is likely to have a dedicated secretary. However, she may occasionally support the rest of his team. If she is lucky enough to be working for a more erudite boss, he will allow her to hire and supervise her own assistants in the form of an administrative assistant and/or a receptionist, as illustrated in figure 11. The secretary in this scenario supervises the administrative assistant and receptionist and oversees and apportions the work from the four managers equitably between them. In this case, the secretary will work exclusively for the director and assist in any overflow from her subordinates when necessary.

Running the Office

A common prerequisite for senior administrative/secretarial positions is the ability to handle anything involving the running of an office. The following is a fragment of a job description stipulating that particular skill:

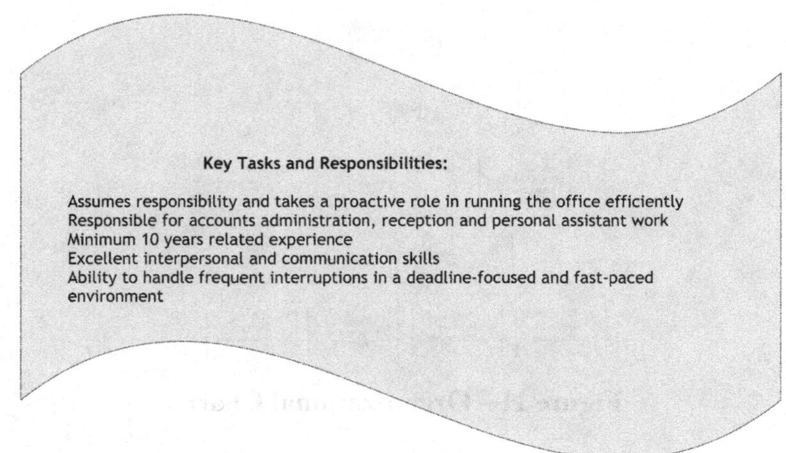

Key Tasks and Responsibilities:
Assumes responsibility and takes a proactive role in running the office efficiently
Responsible for accounts administration, reception and personal assistant work
Minimum 10 years related experience
Excellent interpersonal and communication skills
Ability to handle frequent interruptions in a deadline-focused and fast-paced environment

Figure 12 – Key Tasks and Responsibilities

When a job advertisement has concise wording such as this, the respondent can deduce that the company in question is likely to be a small- to medium-sized firm. A large corporation generally would not have one secretary running the office. Instead, there would be systems and processes in place that smaller firms simply could not afford to introduce.

What Does "Running the Office" Entail?

In the secretarial world, it means that the secretary is the office manager. She oversees everything from ordering stationery, brewing coffee in the morning, stocking up on office supplies, establishing filing procedures and other processes, ensuring smooth and efficient workflow, and managing any junior secretaries, clerks, and receptionists that there may be. Each and every issue that arises within the office is run by the secretary-*cum*-office manager first, or is relegated to her to resolve.

I have had the privilege of being an office manager three different times for three very different firms. In this role I had the responsibility of ensuring that the entire office ran smoothly, which included my regular secretarial responsibilities, acting as fire warden, and ensuring that the company as a whole was adhering to health and safety regulations.

Any building issues or discomfort experienced by the entire staff was my responsibility. In addition, I supervised the junior secretaries and receptionist positions. Other duties tacked on to this role, depending on the size of the company, may include the following:

- filing – establishing and maintaining complex filing systems
- managing and coordinating off-site storage of company records
- balancing accounts and expense books
- managing petty cash and undertaking all the bank runs
- overseeing mail delivery and supervising post office runs
- event planning
- travel planning
- ordering and replenishing stationery and office supplies
- liaising with the information technology group (IT) and service desk

The role of office manager is a great example of what is entailed in running an office and shows just how much responsibility can be assigned to a secretary. The secretary must be highly motivated and possess good judgement and strong interpersonal skills to be successful in this role. In essence, she must resemble an octopus. Such a role demands the ability to handle many different tasks at one time, as well as quick and proactive thinking and action. For instance, I learned in this role that allowing stationery and other office supplies to run out before replenishing them rendered me useless, and such carelessness was viewed as extreme inefficiency on my part. An office manager needs to think on her feet as well as multitask. Most secretaries are office managers in some capacity due to the nature of the work involved. In some cases, it is an unwritten rule that the secretary takes care of certain responsibilities within the office or department, and it is this that essentially makes her an office manager.

For the secretary who aspires to be an office manager, I must give a word of warning. In my experience, some smaller firms or departments will hire an office manager, in part, because their departments are in disarray and they require someone to devise and refine their processes and procedures. An experienced office manager brings order to the chaos and introduces processes where none existed. This can be a thankless job on occasion because some companies are interested only in getting their house in order. Once this has been done, the office manager is sometimes taken for granted and given no opportunity to expand beyond her current role. Several of the office managers I interviewed for this book expressed frustration at the lack of recognition for their hard work and absence of opportunity. In each case, when the secretaries expressed dissatisfaction with their job responsibilities, they were either shown the door or led to believe that they were free to leave. Indeed, I experienced the same ingratitude in those instances when I sought to expand my role beyond the scope of an office manager. When I elected to leave, the companies didn't seem too chagrined but were happy to keep the process improvements that I had implemented in place. This isn't to say that all organizations respond in the same manner. Many value all their human resources and are committed to investing in the office manager's professional development and career goal fulfillment.

Larger firms relegate office management to a department aptly named office services. The office services department will carry out the same responsibilities that fall within the office manager's purview in a smaller firm, such as overseeing stationery supplies for the entire firm, coordinating and delivering mail, overseeing the building and cleaning contractors, and coordinating office moves.

Modern Definitions for Secretaries

Administrative Assistant

Sometime in the mid-1990s, the accepted title for a professional person employed to perform clerical, typing, and varied administrative duties became "administrative assistant." National Secretaries Day, occurring during the aptly named National Secretaries Week, morphed into Administrative Professionals Day/Week in the year 2000. This holiday, observed during the last week in April, was set aside like many other occupation-based holidays as an opportunity for those supported by administrative professionals to pay homage to their magnificent efforts.

The holiday was introduced in 1952 by the International Association of Administrative Professionals (IAAP). According to the IAAP website, the practice was introduced "as an effort to recognize secretaries for their contributions in the workplace, and to attract people to secretarial/ administrative careers."[17]

The title change or clarification made sense, given the expanded job functions that secretaries were undertaking over and above what had been generally recognized as a secretary's role, including, filing, typing and clerical work. The title "administrative assistant" is viewed by many to be less limiting than "secretary," but I made my own views about it clear at the beginning of this chapter.

Executive Secretary/Executive Assistant

This is the title given to secretaries who support senior executives. Executive assistants are required to have at least five to ten years' experience and must demonstrate some business acumen. Superior communication skills are imperative for executive assistants because they are often called upon to represent and speak for the executive in his absence. Unlike administrative assistants, whose focus might be limited to the administrative function, executive assistants are often entrusted with information of a highly confidential nature that requires an elevated level of maturity and experience.

When the executive assistant/secretary has the word "senior" in front of their title, they have reached the pinnacle of their career and the profession. They are highly sought after to provide support at the CEO level and are required to have a cache of superior skills to justify their move to or incumbency in this position. The necessary skill set would normally be acquired through a combination of formal education and at least ten years' working experience. Characteristics of a senior executive assistant/secretary include the following:

17 "Administrative Professionals Week History: Name changed to Administrative Professionals Week," *IAAP*, accessed September 5, 2010, http://www.iaap-hq.org/events/apw/faq.

- A high level of motivation and common sense
- Emotional maturity
- A friendly, approachable, and even disposition
- Impeccable grooming and professionalism
- A polished and astute demeanour
- Exceptional attention to detail
- Personable nature, outstanding people skills, and personal integrity
- Highly developed planning and organization skills
- Ability to perform well under extreme pressure
- Ability to work with minimal supervision
- Excellent writing, editing, and speaking skills
- Numerical literacy
- Discretion, tact, and diplomacy: experience in handling confidential and time-sensitive matters
- Superior computer skills
- A sound understanding of the associated business or industry
- A "can-do" attitude
- A confident personality able to interact with a wide variety of individuals
- A sense of humour

Personal Assistant

As highlighted at the beginning of this chapter, personal assistant is the widely used label for preeminent secretaries in most European countries, particularly Great Britain, but is equivalent to the executive assistant title. Sometimes the advertisements in Europe will use "personal assistant" and "secretary" interchangeably or together (personal assistant/personal secretary). The role of a personal assistant (PA) is no different in its requirements from that of an executive assistant or executive secretary.

Being a personal assistant (PA) in Great Britain and some parts of Europe is highly regarded. In England, PAs announce their profession with great pride and are not only highly paid but also admired. Working in England as a PA is one of the reasons I remained in the profession for as long as I did. I was highly paid, loved what I did for a living, and had wonderful bosses who not only treated me with respect but also pampered me with a great lifestyle. I was very proud to call myself a PA. Sometime in 2007, the Scottish branch of the British Broadcasting Corporation (BBC) commissioned a tongue-in-cheek six-part drama series "following the fortunes of four personal assistants in the city." The series was a humorous but fairly apt depiction of what it is like to be a PA in some parts of Europe – the privilege, power, high pay, glamour, and of course, office life and its inherent politics.[18]

Support personnel for celebrities are also referred to as personal assistants. The New York Celebrity Assistants' organization (NYCA),[19] whose board of directors consists of present and former assistants to prominent celebrities, has an exhaustive list on its website of the skill set required to succeed in that role. However, it is a quote taken from *Vanity Fair* magazine on NYCA's website that most fully captures for me the demands of the role: "All celebrities have an assistant in their lives. That is, if they know how to pick one. You must possess an obsession with lists, a love of the memo form, a head like the Yellow Pages, and a knack for plumbing, mechanics, botany, and simonizing. She is, simply put, the person you'd want to have around after the apocalypse."[20]

Secretarial Salaries

There are many well-paid secretaries, and others who are, unfortunately, not so well paid. The rate of pay for a secretary at any particular level depends on many factors, the principal ones being *location*, *market*, *company*, *manager (boss)*, and *individual*.

Location

Salary bands for secretaries will vary greatly depending on the geographical region.

---

18 *Take a note … BBC Three appoints P.A.s, a new drama series from BBC Scotland, BBC.co.uk*, accessed February 15, 2010, http://www.bbc.co.uk/print/pressoffice/pressreleases/stories/2007/12_december/13/pas.shtml.

19 "NYCA," accessed December 20, 2009, http://nycelebrityassistants.org/.

20 "NYCA in the News," quoted in *Vanity Fair, NYCA.com*, accessed December 20, 2009, http://nycelebrityassistants.org/.

Market

Although most secretaries are paid well above the minimum wage for their region, they are paid according to what the local labour market will bear. Most employers are guided by salary comparisons and surveys conducted in house or externally through the exclusive engagement of national or regional salary survey specialists.

Company

High-profit-margin companies are likely to compensate all their employees at an above-average rate with no exceptions. A small business, non-profit organization, or local government administration cannot compare to a company with, say, $5 billion in revenues. It is possible for a secretary in a high-net-worth company to earn much more than another secretary doing the exact same job in a smaller and lower-net-worth firm.

Manager (Boss)

The manager or boss is the major influence behind a secretary's remuneration package. How well or not a secretary is paid is attributable to both her boss and what I call the luck of the draw. Some secretaries hit the jackpot and find themselves working with highly intelligent bosses who advocate for the value of their secretaries to be recognized. They defend the right to fair and equitable pay for their assistants. Regrettably, such bosses are rare, and few secretaries are fortunate enough to have one.

Individual

Salaries paid to secretaries can also be based on prior experience, qualifications, and performance. Hence two secretaries working for the same company may be compensated at different levels based on performance and other factors.

It might have been easy to quantify the compensation for a secretary twenty years ago because the job function was well defined. However, the post-millennium secretary is compensated according to the above-noted factors (location, market, company, manager, and individual). The lowest-paid secretaries will be compensated well above the minimum wage within their locale, which can vary from country to country and city to city. However, those secretaries who are at the top level can easily command the high end of their earning potential.

In 2004, I responded to an advertisement for an executive assistant based out of New York City, with the pay range listed at $100,000 to $110,000 USD. Not too long after that submission, I noted yet another position in an online advertisement offering a compensation package amounting to $180,000 USD, also in New York City. This is the highest range I have ever seen for this line of work. It is both possible and feasible that a secretary somewhere is paid well above that range, but it should also be noted that salary is always based on one or all of the previously stated five major factors.

In Canada, a number of senior secretaries working in the lucrative oil and gas industries are already in the six-figure salary range when their total compensation package is included. A total compensation package typically refers to base pay, personal allowances, annual bonus, stock options, registered retirement packages, and savings accounts, for which the employer typically matches a percentage of the employee's own contribution, thus providing free cash, and in some cases includes company-paid parking and BlackBerry or cellular phone. If not in the six-figure range, a large number of the senior secretaries in these highly coveted oil and gas sector roles have a salary that hovers just below that mark, and quite often they are paid more than a manager in a smaller firm.

To find out the going rate in your area, perform a search on the Internet for salary surveys conducted specifically for secretaries, or contact your local labour office for the latest statistics and salary guides. Another good source for gauging the salary scale for secretaries in your region is to contact a local employment agency. While some of them do conduct surveys of their own, they always keep abreast of the shifting market trends for secretarial salaries. I recommend visiting websites such as salary.com, payscale.com, or the equivalent in your region, particularly if you want to gauge your own worth or in preparation for a job interview. These sources help educate and keep you informed of the salary trends for secretaries across the board.

The Dress Code for Secretaries

When it comes to personal appearance, secretaries must strive for a balance between comfort and professionalism. It is perfectly acceptable to be stylish or fashionable, as long as it is done in good taste. In my experience, I have found a fair number of organizations are lax about dress codes, which frustrates me as an image consultant. Employees cannot be blamed for wearing something that could be considered inappropriate for work if employers do not institute and enforce definitive dress codes.

The twenty-first century ushered in the business casual style of dress for the workplace. Adoptees of the concept claimed that they were rebelling against the "suited" establishment. This was a noble attempt made by employers to be flexible about dress codes and enable employees to wear comfortable clothing to the office. Unfortunately, many companies jumped on the business casual bandwagon but failed to provide a clear definition of what it meant for their employees. This lack of direction on the employers' part led to confusion and incorrect interpretations by employees. As a result, a number of firms soon abandoned the concept. In my capacity as an image consultant, I focussed a fair portion of my business in the corporate sector on *decoding* what business casual meant for different companies.

Dress Rules for the Elite Secretary

1. *Dress for success*

In the corporate world, your image is the first indicator of your professionalism. Therefore, your professionalism should extend to your wardrobe.

An article that appeared in the UK *Guardian* newspaper was most intriguing to me because the bosses and business owners who were surveyed confirmed the notion that appropriate dress *does* matter. A survey carried out by the HR consultancy firm Reabur ascertained that "other personal traits employers found unappealing included bad dress sense (56 per cent), inappropriate sense of humour (47 per cent), or workers who were simply considered to be unattractive (41per cent)."[21] As ridiculous as this sounds, secretaries everywhere should beware!

Do not confuse being stylish with being sexy. Strive for a look some call "style" and others call "taste," as in having "good taste." Short skirts and décolletage are not in good taste for the office environment – they are distracting and inappropriate. Another example where this confusion arises is with skirts and dresses. Professional secretaries should never wear skirts or dresses that are

- too short – miniskirts/micro minis
- too tight – if it rides up your hips when you sit, it is too tight
- too revealing – any dress/skirt that reveals too much skin (see-through fabric or high front, back or side slits)

Dresses must be suitable for the work environment. Recognize that business attire is essentially different from social attire. That little black dress that you wear when you go out socially is inappropriate for the workplace if it is too short or revealing. Dresses or tops with spaghetti straps should always be paired with a tailored jacket or blazer. The other extreme of casual attire is clothing that is extremely baggy, such as sweatpants and tracksuits, which are inappropriate for the office and do not convey professionalism. Capri pants should also be avoided – they are not appropriate for the office.

You can build a good core work wardrobe using tailored pieces as the foundation. In my opinion, tailored pieces function as "anchors" for your wardrobe because they coordinate well with other, less formal garments.

---

21 Graham Snowdon, "How do you rank on personal hygiene?" *The Guardian*, accessed December 5, 2010, http://www.guardian.co.uk/money/blog/2010/sep/23/personal-hygiene-bad-habits?

For example, pairing a tailored jacket with a summer dress or skirt transforms it into a more business-appropriate outfit.

For a guaranteed investment, male secretaries should endeavour to buy quality tailored suits, trousers, blazers, and sport jackets rather than investing in a large quantity of lesser quality clothing.

If you are uncertain about the suitability of an outfit for the work environment, stand in front of a full-length mirror and ask yourself the following questions:

- How do I want to be perceived today?
- What image do I want to portray?
- Who is my audience/who will I come into contact with today? Clients, board members, executives, colleagues?
- Am I dressing in accordance with the corporate dress code?
- Does my outfit convey professionalism?

If you cannot definitively say your attire is suitable as defined by your company dress code, I would suggest that you reconsider wearing it. Remember, the more skin you show, the less professional you appear to be. Strive for a refined, elegant appearance. When consulting with my clients on image matters, I often tell them, "*You* and *you alone* decide exactly how you want to be perceived in the world."

2. *Observe proper fit*

There is nothing worse than an ill-fitting outfit. Dressing well also means wearing clothes that fit properly. Irrespective of the cost, label, fabric, or colour of your clothing, a poor fit will ruin the look. Dress pants should fit properly and not be too tight in the crotch or seat area. Jackets should fit as though they were custom made for you, especially in the shoulders. Buttons on your blouse or shirt shouldn't pull. When shopping for clothing, use size labels as a guide only; remember, sizes vary according to the brand/label/designer. Be prepared to have your clothes altered. Seamstresses are not in the business of fixing hemlines alone; they can be instrumental in achieving that perfect fit.

Male secretaries should pay attention to jacket sleeve length (the right fit allows for a quarter to half an inch of shirt cuff to show) and ensure the shoulders and back fit properly.

Trousers should hang well and not sag or be tight around the seat area. Wearing slightly short trousers is considered youthful and fashionable, but it makes men who are already short appear even shorter. Trousers should break at the top of the shoes and just brush the heel. Male secretaries must take note of the vicissitudes of fashion because trouser styles will vary from season to season. Flat fronts might be all the rage in one season, and the next, one or two pleats might be the "in" thing.

3. *Invest in a tailored business suit*

Invest in a good quality pant/skirt/dress suit in darker hues suited to your skin tone.

If you own just one suit, then reserve it for those times when you are required to attend important or formal meetings at work. Suits are symbols of authority, so make sure you wear a suit to every job interview.

Do not break up your suits by repeatedly wearing the pant without the jacket. The regular laundering will affect the quality and hue of the fabric, and you will wear out the pants first. If funds are available, male secretaries should buy two pairs of pants with each matching jacket, since they tend to wear out first.

Do remember that women's fashion is constantly evolving. Try to keep up with current fashion trends, and update your wardrobe regularly. Wearing an extremely dated suit is as much a fashion faux pas as donning inappropriate attire.

4. *Know your colours*

Wear the right colours for your skin complexion. Do not be misled into thinking that every person can wear any colour they want. Image consultants will be the first to tell you that wearing the right colours for your personal colouring (skin, hair, and eyes) can transform the way you look, and they are correct. Wearing clothes in your best colours will positively enhance your skin tone, giving you a more radiant and vibrant complexion. Wearing the wrong colours has the opposite effect. A dull, tired complexion can result from wearing the wrong colours close to the skin.

For business attire, women are fortunate because they have more colour options than men. The key is in striking the right tone and balance in your colour choices. Bold colours and prints may not serve you well unless you know how to coordinate them to achieve a professional look.

5. *Build a capsule wardrobe*

Build a wardrobe that works! Invest in separates that are interchangeable and coordinate well with the rest of your wardrobe. Capsule wardrobes are also known as "wardrobe clusters" and enable you to create a variety of outfits using a few colour-coordinated pieces. Wardrobe basics such as the classic white shirt, black dress pants, a tailored skirt, and sports jacket are great starting points for building a suitable capsule for your work wardrobe. You can build your wardrobe using one capsule as the foundation, or you can create wardrobe clusters for specific occasions to suit your lifestyle.

With regards to colour, male secretaries should note the rules regarding socks:

- Match your socks to your trousers, but choose socks that coordinate with both your trousers and shoes. In other words, try to keep your trousers, socks, and shoes in the same colour family.
- Socks worn with slightly shorter trousers need to be fairly long (knee high) to avoid subjecting onlookers to visible bare flesh between the socks and the trousers when sitting cross-legged.

6. *Observe the psychology of clothes*

Avoid wearing anything that doesn't feel authentic to you, and make sure that you don't copy someone else's *personal* style. When you wear clothes that make you feel uncomfortable, your unease is evident to those who are observant. Similarly, it is of no use to copy others for the sake of competing with them – you will always lose! You must develop your own personal style that complements your body type, personal colouring, personality, profession, lifestyle, and budget. If you take these principles into consideration when you are shopping or dressing for work, you will be happy with the way you look. The self-assurance derived from that will filter into other facets of your life. More importantly, your confidence will positively affect your deportment, and others will perceive you as authentic.

7. *Accessories complete the outfit*

Do remember that accessories are not limited to just earrings and a watch. An accessory is a small article or item of clothing carried or worn to complement an outfit. Shoes, handbags, watch, belts, hosiery, and gloves are all part of the accessory family. For secretaries in particular, I would advise that you maintain your professional look by avoiding

- any more than one ring per hand
- clunky, large, gaudy earrings, bracelets, and neck chains
- an oversized handbag or briefcase
- fishnet stockings
- oversized or overly trendy spectacles

8. *Shoes*

Shoes are an accessory, but they deserve special mention. Depending on your office dress code, sandals, evening-style stilettos, running shoes, flip-flops, and certain styles of open-toed shoes should be avoided. Some offices allow women to wear mules and others allow sandals in the summer, but always follow and abide by your company's dress code.

If you want to maintain a professional look as a secretary and *there is no definitive dress code in your office*, I would suggest that

- You never wear sandals to work – no one wants to see all your toes in the office!
- Peep-toes and sling-backs are the exception to this rule. However, both styles do require that you get a pedicure before wearing them.

- Sling-backs are acceptable because they are closed in the front with a sandal style strap around the heel.
- Peep-toes are borderline acceptable, depending on the style of the shoe and the condition of your feet. Some peep-toe shoes are acceptable not only because they look semi-professional but also because the shoe may only expose a small surface of your big toe. Other styles have a very narrow opening at the front that does not actually expose any of your toes.
- For a strictly professional look, open-toed shoes of any kind should be avoided in a corporate environment.
- If you must wear high-heeled pumps (also known as court shoes) to work, as I do, please make sure that you can actually walk in them. Furthermore, make certain that the shoes in question are comfortable enough for you to wear the entire work day. If you are tempted to take off your shoes, then keep a pair of ballet flats or lower-heeled pumps in your office to switch to in emergencies.
- Take care of your shoes! The "down look" is not just unflattering, it is another fashion faux pas. Find a good cobbler and have your shoes regularly repaired to avoid hobbling around with a missing heel.
- Shoes can break unexpectedly, or you could lose a perfectly good heel. Be prepared for emergencies by keeping a spare pair of shoes in your office.
- Assuming you wear professional business attire, always wear shoes that complement your outfit.
- For men, black and brown are the only acceptable shoe colours for a business environment. Even so, shoes and belts signify a lot about a man and his personal style. The next time you encounter what you consider to be a well-dressed man, observe where your focus goes. Certainly you might scrutinize his suit, trousers or shirt colour and condition, but your eye will naturally land on his waistline (belt) and feet (shoes). That observation will lead you to your own perceptions about the individual. For men, shoes and belts complete the outfit.

9. *Practice impeccable grooming*

The aforementioned *Guardian* article that discussed a survey carried out by HR consultancy firm Reabur also posed a question about grooming and personal hygiene to a group of bosses and business owners. According to the survey results, "Sixty-eight per cent of business owners agreed that putting aside experience and qualifications, poor personal hygiene would be the main factor in deciding whether to employ someone or not."[22]

Of course, good personal hygiene and grooming is not just incumbent on the secretary. Secretaries work in close proximity with their bosses, so they should also practice impeccable grooming and personal hygiene.

Grooming Tips for the Elite Secretary

Besides the obvious personal hygiene that we must all attend to (hair, make-up, oral hygiene, deodorant, etc.) you may find these tips useful:

- Hanging a garment in a steamy bathroom can help minimize wrinkles like a professional steamer. However, if you can, it is wise to invest in a professional clothes steamer, as it will save you money on dry cleaning costs.
- Most people view manicures and pedicures as luxuries. I view them as essential for both men and women. Even if you disagree with the classification of luxury versus essential, what is wrong with regularly pampering yourself in order to look your best?
- That first smile could make all the difference in a public profession like secretarial. Visit your dentist regularly, and if you aren't confident in your smile, consider investing in cosmetic dentistry – the return on your investment could improve your chances of winning your dream six-figure job.

Especially for Women:

- Invest in a good bra, as an ill-fitting one will ruin an outfit. Regardless of how nice your clothes may be, a bra riding up your back or providing minimal support will negate all your best efforts in achieving that polished look.
- When laundering white tops, always check the collars and under the arms for perspiration stains. If the stains are obvious and permanent, discard and replace.

---

22 Snowdon, Graham. "How do you rank on personal hygiene?" *The Guardian*. Accessed December 5, 2010, http://www.guardian.co.uk/money/blog/2010/sep/23/personal-hygiene-bad-habits?INTCMP=SRCH.

Especially for Men:

- Bowties have no business in the office, unless you are just passing through or getting dressed in preparation to attend a black tie/formal evening event.
- When laundering white shirts, always check under the arms for perspiration stains. If the stains are obvious and permanent, discard and replace.
- Avoid loading your back trouser pocket with keys and a heavy wallet, as it ruins the shape of the garment.

While I was conducting my research on corporate dress codes, an HR executive forwarded to me what she described as a "sample of her company's dress guidelines."[23] What I liked the most about this partial dress code policy was how appropriate and inappropriate clothing were clearly defined (see figure 13).

23 Company name and source is confidential.

Figure 13 - Sample Office Dress Code Policy

ITEM	APPROPRIATE	INAPPROPRIATE
Pants and pantsuits	• Tailored dress/Capri pants made of cotton, polyester, wool, etc.	• Torn or ripped denim, leggings, sweatpants, tracksuits, jogging pants, shorts, and overalls
Skirts and dresses	• Tailored dresses and skirts: knee length or longer	• Mini/short skirts and spaghetti-strap dresses
Shirts, tops, blouses	• Dress shirts/sweaters, turtlenecks, collared shirts, blouses, and golf shirts	• Spaghetti-strap tank tops, crop tops, halter tops, low-cut/revealing tops, sweatshirts, casual T-shirts, and shirts displaying racist or similarly offensive messages, words, terms, slogans, pictures, or cartoons
Jackets	• Tailored, suit, or sport jackets, blazers	• Flashy, bright collared leathers and metallics
Shoes	• Dress shoes, conservative walking shoes, pumps, loafers, boots, flats, dress heels	• Dilapidated footwear, Ugg™ boots, running or athletic-style shoes, flip-flops, slippers, sandals
Jewellery, make-up, perfume, and cologne	• Be considerate of other people's sensitivities to scented products. Use of scents should be subtle and in good taste.	• Heavily plied make-up, perfume, and cologne
<u>Please note</u> that this is just an example of one organization's dress code policy. *While not exhaustive, this dress code clearly defines appropriate vs. inappropriate clothing at this particular firm.* Company name and source is confidential.		

When a client encounters an inappropriately dressed secretary, he or she may walk away with a less favourable image of the organization as a whole. Although employees are individuals with their own personal image preferences, they should conform to whatever their company defines as the preferred corporate image.

In the absence of a formal dress code, secretaries should observe the way their boss and other senior executives dress. Certain kinds of organizations tend to be quite formal (such as law firms), and if you choose to show up for work in frilly, loud prints, busy patterns, and dated suits, you are not going to be taken seriously. Image does matter, so secretaries must always present themselves professionally. Even if you are good at your job, a less-than-polished personal appearance could hurt your credibility and hinder your career progression.

The adage "dress for the job you want" is certainly applicable to secretaries. My advice for secretaries who struggle in this area is to aspire for a look that lies somewhere between business formal and business casual. Business formal comprises a tailored matching suit with a tie for men and a tailored matching dress/skirt/pant suit for women. It is not a bad idea to discuss dress code with your boss, particularly at the beginning of your working relationship. If none of these options are available to you, use the guidelines that I provided in chapter 3, in the section titled "Interview Dress Guide for Women" and also observe the section "Dress Rules for the Elite Secretary" in this chapter.

If your boss doesn't dress professionally, that is not your problem – you must still present yourself professionally and maintain the high standard of an elite secretary.

To build a good working wardrobe, seek the assistance of an image consultant or stylist. While doing so, remember that you must tailor your wardrobe to the industry you are part of and to your position within the firm. If you have special considerations such as a requirement to incorporate traditional or religious clothing items into your wardrobe, then a discussion with your boss and human resources advisor is warranted.

Summary

- Secretaries are the cornerstone of many organizations; highly proficient, experienced multitaskers, they are masters at what they do.
- Many executives recognize and appreciate the value a "super secretary" brings to the organization and to the smooth running of their offices.
- Loyalty, discretion, tact and an unflappable "can-do" attitude are essential qualities for any secretary.
- Some secretaries are averse to running errands and making coffee for the boss. To eliminate surprises, a secretary needs to thoroughly review the job description prior to accepting a job offer.
- The secretarial function continues to evolve with the times. Secretaries need to stay abreast of technological advances in their profession.
- Study the organization chart of your own company to understand how crucial your role is to the operational structure.
- There are many definitions for secretaries based on their level of experience, their skill, and their manager's rank in the organization.
- Male secretaries do exist and are no longer a novelty.
- Secretaries are typically compensated well above the minimum wage for their region. However, their total remuneration package is influenced by the location of the country and city where they happen to be, whatever the local market will bear, the company itself and what scale it chooses to set for the role.
- When a secretary is also required to be an "office manager," she has the all-encompassing role of running the office which, in part, entails establishing and overseeing all administrative processes for the company.
- Larger firms will typically institute an office services department instead of hiring an office manager for the same role. In other words, larger firms would not employ an office

manager but an office services manager, whose army of staff would tackle everything that would fall within the purview of an office manager in a smaller firm.

- Remember, you determine how you want to be perceived by how you present yourself to the world.

Chapter 7: The Secretary and the Modern Office

The office environment of 1975 was markedly different from the office environment of 2005 and beyond. Technological advances are inevitable, but the fundamentals that make the office effective have been carried forward consistently and are inextricably tied to the secretarial function. The "office" will continue to evolve.

Understanding the job function and its expectations at the various levels of management is important, but knowing how to comport yourself in the workplace is even more important.

There are rules to be followed, etiquette for every circumstance and procedural guidelines that are rarely communicated to a newcomer either because there has been an oversight or because the employer assumes the secretary is already aware of the etiquette.

The Modern Office

The modern secretary must have an awareness and understanding of these key components in order to be successful in her position:

1. Organizational structure
2. Organizational culture
3. Company policies, procedures, and business practices

How these various components are arranged depends on the size of an organization. Being fully conversant with them provides a crucial starting point for a secretary to build upon.

To be successful in the modern office, you must continuously seek ways to simplify the work processes in your sphere of influence.

Business Conduct and Etiquette

1. Treat everyone fairly. Even though you will encounter people with no scruples, never stoop to their level. Everyone you do business with is entitled to fair and even-handed treatment.
2. Maintain a level of maturity in all your dealings with co-workers, visitors, and clients both internal and external.
3. Attitude is everything. Treat others as you would like to be treated.
4. Never make misrepresentations to anyone. If you believe that another person may have misunderstood your meaning, promptly correct him or her. Attempts to undermine others are unadvisable and may backfire.
5. In order to foster lasting relationships, be ethical in all your dealings. Honesty is integral to ethical behaviour.
6. Avoid being the cause of office conflict, discord, or disharmony.
7. Own up to your mistakes rather than trying to deflect them onto someone else.
8. Be tactful when handling dubious situations and conflicts. Make sure to use proper reporting channels even if it isn't advantageous for you to do so.
9. Do not treat the office environment as a school playground. Professionalism should always guide your conduct.
10. Keep your emotions in check and avoid introducing personal feelings or similar inclinations into business matters. Maintain your integrity.

Top Ten Rules of Office Etiquette

1. Only in those instances where you do not want to be disturbed or are tending to confidential business matters should you work behind closed doors. However, be sure to close your office door when conducting meetings or taking part in a conference call so as not to disturb others.
2. Never ever intentionally slam your door! This is not only inconsiderate but extremely arrogant.

3. Strive to keep a tidy office.
4. Always invite a visitor to sit down.
5. When visiting someone else's office, if you observe that they are on the telephone, come back at another time rather than lingering around outside.
6. Never barge into someone's office uninvited, even if it is your boss; always knock before entering.
7. Never borrow something from another person's office in his absence or without his permission.
8. As a secretary, you will enter your boss's office numerous times in the course of a day; however, do take the time to establish access guidelines at the beginning of the working relationship.
9. Some bosses do not like having papers or other items placed on their chair. Always check with your boss for his preference. If your boss has an "in" tray, use it.
10. If you must interrupt a meeting, write the urgent message or reason for the interruption on a piece of paper, knock on the door, and hand the note to your boss rather than verbally conveying the message to him, which could be a breach of confidence.

Top Ten Rules of Cubicle Etiquette

1. Remember that it is difficult enough to work in a cubicle without having your privacy invaded.
2. Be courteous and keep your voice down while carrying on a conversation with someone in your cubicle, or take your conversation elsewhere.
3. Gauge your voice's volume or pitch while talking on the telephone; it is advisable to use a headset. Furthermore, set your telephone ringer to a low volume.
4. Whenever you leave your desk, activate your voice mail so that your telephone doesn't persistently ring and disturb those in surrounding cubicles.
5. Cellular phones should be set to vibrate or low volume.

6. If you cannot mimic a knock due to the cubicle construction, announce yourself at the doorway and ask the cubicle owner if it is a good time to meet.
7. Conversely, if you are the cubicle owner and do not want to be disturbed, it is helpful to post a "please do not disturb" sign at the entrance.
8. Never borrow something from an individual's cubicle in his absence or without his permission.
9. If you must carry on an impromptu meeting in a hallway or in the vicinity of someone's cubicle, be courteous and lower your voice, or take the meeting elsewhere.
10. Foods with a strong door should be eaten in the kitchen, break room, or vacant meeting room unless it is lunchtime and everyone else is eating or gone to lunch; if you must eat foods with a strong door at your desk outside these hours, be courteous and warn those working around you.

Telephone Etiquette

This instrument is perhaps the most important one in the modern office. It is the lifeline of all operations and deserves mention in this and every book that is dedicated to office procedures. While most trained secretaries will be conversant with the importance of the telephone in the business world, a reminder is warranted even to the veterans of this profession.

First impressions are derived on the telephone as well as in person. As a secretary, it is important to remember this fact each and every time you lift up the receiver to answer the telephone.

Many books and etiquette instructors will advise you to smile first before picking up the telephone, but few people remember to do that. Here are the key components for appropriate use of the telephone:

Making a telephone call

1. When the person you are calling answers, say, "Good morning," "Good afternoon," "Good evening," or "Hello," depending on the time of your call.
2. Introduce yourself either by your first name if you are known to the other party, or by stating your full name and the company you represent.
3. Inform the person of why you are calling and promptly get to the point, thus respecting the value of his or her time.
4. Avoid making personal calls during business hours (even if you see others doing so), except in emergencies. If you must call a family member, do so during your breaks, but keep the calls brief. Long, personal chats with girlfriends to share gossip should be carried out on your personal phone outside office hours.
5. Be aware of the volume of your voice and observe cubicle and office etiquette; do not raise your voice so as to disturb other employees. Be respectful of others and curb your volume appropriately. If you feel uncertain about this, approach other employees and verify that the volume of your voice while on the telephone does not disturb or distract. Polite employees may not directly inform you in an effort not to hurt your feelings. However, if you have one person you do trust to tell you the truth, ask her to gauge your voice while on the telephone and to tell you honestly if she could hear the conversation.
6. To end a call, thank the person for his time and gently hang up.

Answering the telephone

1. Answer by the third ring and immediately identify yourself with a friendly but warm and professional tone.
2. Keep it simple by stating your first and last name followed by "good morning" or "good afternoon." ("Susan Smith, good morning.") There is no need to postscript your greeting with "speaking." It is obvious that you are speaking!

3. Some organizations may prefer that you also state your department so that the caller is immediately made aware that he has reached the correct person. In this case, you again state your full name and then simply add the department name: "Susan Smith, Finance Department, good morning."
4. Occasions will arise when you may be required to pick up your boss's personal line, and this is the exception to the rule, because you must inform the caller that although he has reached the right number, a stranger is taking the call. The appropriate greeting in this case would be, "Office of the President, this is Amanda Wright" or "Mr. Edward's office, this is Amanda Wright."
5. The appropriate response for a secretary when her boss is unable to accept a call is, "I am sorry, he is in (or at) a meeting. May I take a message for him?" It is not always necessary to inform the caller exactly where your boss is or what he is up to, unless it is the head of the organization on the line or a member of his immediate family in an emergency situation. The correct response to everyone is, "I am sorry, he is in a meeting at the moment," or "I am afraid he has left the office for an off-site meeting. Could I take a message for him?" Never state that you do not know where he is or that he never bothered to inform you of his movements, even if it's true. Be courteous on the phone always and without exception.
6. When screening calls, always watch your tone of voice for congeniality. If there are certain people your boss does not want to talk to, he will tell you. However, that is not a license to be rude to the caller. Simply advise the caller that your boss is unavailable, then find out if you can assist or take a message. Regular callers or personal friends of your boss may expect you to recognize their voices over time. However, unless your boss stipulates that you can interrupt him for that particular caller, offer to take a message. Right from the beginning of your relationship, request a list from your boss of his personal

friends and family members and clarify the rules about how to handle calls from those people.

7. Never place anyone on hold without obtaining his permission to do so. Say, "I am afraid his line is busy at the moment, would you like to hold or leave a message?" If the caller chooses to hold, you must periodically check if he wishes to continue holding.
8. During business hours, your line must be answered by a live person. If you must step away from your desk, there should be a back-up person to man your line for you, or a well-scripted and informative voice mail greeting recorded on your telephone. (More about voice mail later in this chapter.)
9. Do not multitask or eat while talking on the telephone. It is not only rude but also trivializes the call and conveys a sense of disrespect to the other party. Quite often the caller can sense the fact that you are doing something else while talking to him. Many secretaries have a habit of cradling the receiver between their neck and ear and carrying on a conversation while their fingers bash at the keyboard incessantly at the same time. This is rude behaviour that should be avoided by all professional secretaries. If you are looking up something on the computer for the caller, ask if you can place him on hold while you retrieve the information, or use the mouse to perform a search on his behalf.
10. Never answer someone else's personal phone (desk, home, mobile) unless he asks you to do so.

Taking Messages

As the secretary, your role is to make your manager's life a little easier. You are of no assistance to your manager if you are not responsible when taking telephone messages. Telephone messages are another integral part of the secretary's portfolio, and great care must go into this activity. Every manager or executive expects common sense from his secretary where telephone messages are concerned and needs specific information in order for a telephone message to be complete.

- Who called? Provide the full name and the organization the caller represents.
- When did they call? Provide the date and the exact time of the call.
- What was the purpose of the call? Provide any specific message relayed.
- What is their telephone number? No matter how many times a person has called in the past, you must verify his number and whether it is his office number or mobile number where he can be reached.

Voice Mail

1. Business voice mail greetings should be professional and succinct. They should state the company name, your name, your availability (for the day or week – but only if you are not likely to forget to update this information regularly), and an invitation to the caller to leave a message.
2. When leaving a message on someone else's voice mail, speak slowly, clearly enunciating your words, especially if you have an accent that is foreign to the region. If you are unknown to the person or if you have an unusual last name, it is helpful to spell it out.
3. Avoid leaving long messages on business voice mails. Leave a very brief message and your contact number stating what you are calling about and how the person may contact you.
4. Remember to extend the same courtesy on voice mail as you would like to receive.

Electronic Mail

Equally important in the communications arena is electronic mail. With the arrival of the millennium came the prevalence of e-mail as a communication tool. The adoption of this method of communication en masse has fostered a lapse in etiquette and common courtesy. Remember to extend the same courtesy and follow the same guidelines when communicating via e-mail as you would in a face-to-face encounter or regular mail.

E-mail Etiquette

1. Always state the subject or purpose of your e-mail in the subject box. It is not only courteous but also helps the other party manage their e-mail account effectively, whether they file the message for future use, forward it to the appropriate party to act on, or determine if they need to address it immediately themselves.
2. Address the person you are writing with a greeting, such as "Hi, Susan" (if she is known to you), or "Good morning/Dear Mr. or Ms. Jones" (if unknown to you), just as you would do in formal correspondence.
3. Refrain from spelling out words in capital letters in an e-mail message. This is interpreted as anger or shouting.
4. Do not use your business e-mail account for personal use. To do so would abuse the privilege your employer has extended to you. Furthermore, regardless of your attempts to delete them, business e-mails are kept due to legal considerations and will remain on the company's server for a very long time.
5. Limit the practice of forwarding chain letters and an excessive number of crude or vulgar jokes. These e-mails may contain viruses that can harm the company's network and could potentially damage your employer's computer or your own.
6. Do not use your business e-mail to carry on long, drawn-out correspondence about personal matters such as love affairs, personal business ventures, and other spurious interactions that are unrelated to the function of your job. If you bring a personal smart phone to work, use a personal account to read e-mails (for example, Gmail), but it's important to avoid these types of exchanges during work hours.
7. Refrain from using vulgar language in any business e-mail.
8. If you are sending an e-mail externally to a number of people who do not know each other, the onus is on you to protect their privacy by using the "blind copy" feature. Revealing an individual's e-mail address to others without her express permission is a betrayal of her trust.

9. None of the messages you send using your business e-mail account should contain profanity or defamatory statements about your employer.
10. Endeavour to reply to e-mails within forty-eight hours of receipt. If you are going to be away for longer than forty-eight hours, it is courteous to activate the "out of office assistant" or "instant reply" feature on your e-mail to warn senders about your extended absence.
11. If you are upset about the behavior of a coworker and want to express this in an e-mail, sleep on the e-mail overnight before sending it, as hot emotions can lead people to write regrettable correspondence.

Internet Use

Keep in mind that, as with e-mail, access to the Internet is a privilege bestowed upon you by your employer. Most companies employ analysts whose job description is to vet and log Internet usage throughout the company. Unbeknownst to most employees, some companies regularly audit Internet use by their staff – an enlightening exercise for the employer on many levels. While some employers will ignore harmless Internet browsing conducted for informative, referential, or educational purposes, be aware that they log all your movements online. Disobeying your company's Internet policy or using your computer inappropriately could undermine your career and future opportunities.

Proprietary Information

Secretaries are privy to confidential company information. In fact, most employers request that you sign a non-disclosure agreement (NDA) upon accepting a job offer. This is not something to be taken lightly, for as a secretary to a lawyer, finance executive, marketing executive, human resources executive, or CEO, you are entrusted with extremely sensitive information that is known as "intellectual property." Accidental, inadvertent, or intentional disclosure of any information related to your job is a breach of the NDA, is illegal, and could land you in jail.

In 2006, the media reported that an executive administrative assistant (EA) employed by Coca-Cola allegedly compromised the high regard and unquestionable trust most employers give to their secretarial staff. The EA was arrested along with two others on July 5, 2006, for allegedly stealing confidential information (she was observed on surveillance video stuffing proprietary information into her handbag) and attempting to sell her employer's drink recipes and trade secrets for $1.5 million USD![24] Her previous employer, Coca-Cola, was quoted in the piece as stating that "the breach of trust was difficult to accept." Indeed, this kind of behaviour is not normally associated with secretaries and would be difficult for any well-trained and well-intentioned secretary to comprehend. I have no idea where this EA was trained or how she allegedly came to be in such a criminal frame of mind, but her behaviour is in no way representative of the majority in this profession.

Filing

Filing systems vary according to industry and area. Legal firms require specialized filing systems, and the majority of legal secretaries acquire the associated training within their legal secretarial course. Most secretaries, if they are being honest, will express an innate loathing of this part of their job, particularly because it is so mundane and repetitious. However, once an organized system is in place it makes future filing exercises easier. Filing is an intrinsic element of secretarial work.

All well-trained secretaries will have covered the filing basics within their secretarial courses. Most come into a new job knowing full well that some serious filing will be involved. The incoming secretary will need to establish a filing process or procedure that she is comfortable with, one which will blend in with the existing process or will be even simpler.

---

24 "Two Ex-Coke Workers Sentenced in Pepsi Plot Deal." CNN.com, accessed June 25, 2011, http://www.cnn.com/2007/LAW/05/23/coca.cola.sentencing.

Whether you work in the legal sector, a hospital environment, or the corporate sector, filing must be done well or business operations will be hampered, and this in turn will cast doubt on your capability and competence. The most important thing to remember about filing is that it should be set up in a manner that makes document retrieval effortless. When the boss requests a file from his secretary, it should take her no more than a minute or two to retrieve it. It should be just as easy for anyone sitting in for the secretary to understand the filing system and retrieve files easily.

Filing Dos and Don'ts

1. *Make it simple*

It is pointless to create a complicated filing system if it is going to create more work for someone each time she needs a file. The secretary and her boss or others using the system should be able to pull the file they need with minimal effort. Alphabetical filing systems are by far the best and the easiest to maintain.

2. *Make it a team effort*

Whether you work for one or more bosses, spend some time studying the business at hand and determine the most logical filing system for the environment. It isn't just about the secretary. Others should be able to retrieve files in the secretary's absence. A smart secretary walking into a new job will do her own research by conversing with those who use the filing system and determining the challenges they face with the current system and what they would like to see in a new system.

3. *Learn the business*

In order to understand what you are filing and the best possible system for the business at hand, try to maintain some familiarity and an understanding of what is happening in the files by reading memos and letters. Take responsibility for checking the status of documents on file, bring to the attention of your boss any discrepancies you catch on the files, and engage in a dialogue, all in an effort to learn the business.

4. *Do it now*

Procrastination where filing is concerned can lead to a secretary's downfall. It not only looks incompetent but can also have serious repercussions for the secretary if important papers are left loose and unfiled and are lost. It also creates more work for the secretary than is necessary. Filing papers immediately cuts down on time and the mundane nature of the activity.

5. *Labelling and colour coordination*

Files should be neat and clearly labelled for ease of retrieval. Labelling also minimizes the misfiling and loss of documents. If you use labels on files, ensure that they are secure or use an adhesive. Colour coding is a great idea, as long as it is consistent.

6. *Neatness matters*

Keep files neat and tidy—no "dog ears." Never use paper clips to secure or connect pages within a file. Instead, staple pages on the right side, or use bulldog clips for larger documents. Do not leave items loose in the file. Take care not to misfile, as it is careless and unprofessional.

7. *File check-out system*

It is extremely important to create a file check-out system. This is a method for tracking the movements of a file if multiple people within a department are using the same filing system. A competent secretary never wants to look incompetent because she doesn't know who has a certain file.

8. *Reminder and "brought forward" files*

Do set up a separate filing system for all the files that need to be flagged to your manager for action. This is a very important part of a secretary's job: the boss is allowed to forget things but secretaries are not!

9. *Use the brought forward or reminder filing system*

This is necessary for all the papers and documents that your boss asks you to flag for a future date as well as for your own personal observations of where a reminder might be warranted. This type of system is normally set up using day, month, and future outlook categories, and as such must be reviewed each and every day by the secretary and immediately acted upon by the secretary or her boss, and then filed in the normal channels. This prevents things from falling through the cracks.

10. *Index it*

Once your filing system is up and running, create an index to correspond with the system and keep it in a place where others can find it. An index is crucial, since in the event of your unexpected absence, business must go on.

The secretary must ensure that, in addition to a functional filing system, she has a well-developed process for off-site storage of archived records. The guidelines for the number of years that records must be kept before they are destroyed will vary from country to country and industry to industry. It is the secretary's responsibility to be conversant with the recommended guidelines for record-keeping in her particular field. The secretary must institute a process that makes the retrieval of archived records simple and easy for others to carry out in her absence. All records kept off site must be catalogued for ease of retrieval.

Time Management and Organizational Skills

It is the nature of the secretarial work to multitask. Learning to do so is vital and, if you find it difficult to do more than one task at a time, this may not be the career for you. Multitasking involves doing more than one task at a time without becoming distracted, flustered, or annoyed. A secretary must be able to exercise initiative and work in an organized and methodical manner while exhibiting an ability to manage multiple tasks. The more experienced the secretary, the greater the expectation is that she will ramp up her efficiency in the face of competing priorities and stringent deadlines. Employers are constantly on the lookout for that rare talent that exhibits consummate professionalism under extreme pressure and an unfailing ability to produce high-quality work while attending to several matters at a time.

Time management does not mean one is constantly flustered or irritated about the lack of time to fulfil responsibilities and meet looming deadlines. Such displays indicate inexperience, inadequate training, an undesirable attitude, as well as a lack of professionalism. You must have a process in place for determining how you use time and a way to determine whether the process is effective. Consider and answer the following questions first:

1. How many hours a day are you at work?
2. Do you work seven and a half or eight hours a day?
3. Do you normally take a lunch break?
4. How do you typically spend the first half of the day?
5. During which time slots are you most and least productive? Why? How can you improve upon that so that you accomplish your daily goals?
6. What resources or tools do you use to manage your time and balance your tasks?
7. Do you stay organized when you are under pressure, or does chaos prevail?

Why is it important to examine the total number of hours you are at work? When discussing time management, it is important to have a complete picture of the time available and the cost to both the organization and yourself of your unproductive moments. We need to know what we are working with before instituting processes or solutions to counter time waste. Are we working with eight hours, seven and a half hours, or fewer?

Most employers implore their staff to take a lunch break because they know that the break is necessary to refresh the employee's mind so that they are even more productive for the remaining three or four hours of the day. Not taking a lunch break is counterproductive and could give your employer the impression that you are a poor planner and are unable to prioritize tasks or cope with the workload. Your employer might also interpret this as incompetence, or he may assume that you are frittering time away on matters that aren't work related. When attempting to manage your time effectively, you must examine workflow both before and after lunch.

- What time of day is the best to respond to e-mails and voice mails?

- What time of day is best to do filing?
- Do you distinguish between "important" and "urgent" priorities?

Maximize your impact by focusing on what is important. Remember that any time spent planning will save you double the time, if not more, by making you more productive. Planning saves you time in the long run. Always reserve time on your calendar to plan your day, week, and month.

Allow yourself some personal time to catch up on completing pet projects, returning calls, or following up on other matters, and guard this time jealously, as it is important to keep you sane and on target. At the same time, you must always ask yourself, "Is this the best use of my time right now?" and be prepared to adapt and adjust your time to the situation at hand.

When your priorities are challenged or revised, clarify whether a task is important or urgent.

Important versus Urgent

1. To qualify as important, the task or activity must have a tangible, beneficial result and be attributable to organizational goals and objectives.
2. Urgent matters are non-negotiable. A task or activity that is described as "urgent" requires immediate attention. *Urgent means now*!

Do you have a tool or resource that assists you in managing your time so you can meet your goals and deadlines? Something that aids your ability to be effective and eliminates any possible time traps during the course of your day?

Throughout my career, I managed my time according to the following criteria:

1. Plan
2. Prioritize
3. Action

This method, which I called the PPA method of time management, was highly effective when incorporated into a daily "To Do" list. To incorporate the PPA method into a To Do List, I created a list of all that I needed to accomplish within a set time frame (see figure 14).

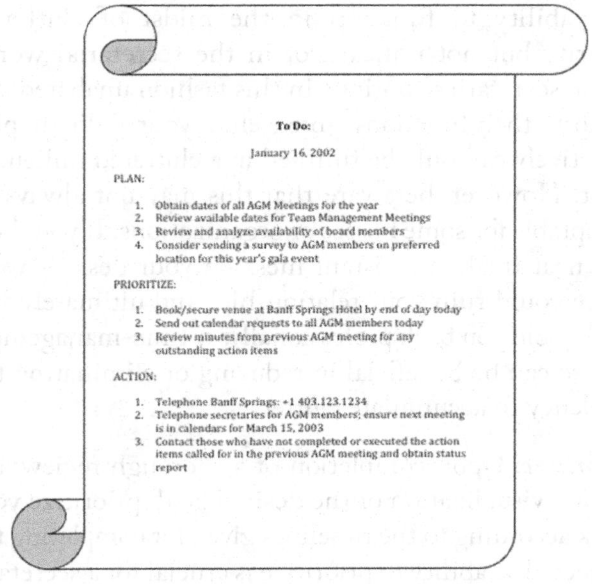

To Do:

January 16, 2002

PLAN:

1. Obtain dates of all AGM Meetings for the year
2. Review available dates for Team Management Meetings
3. Review and analyze availability of board members
4. Consider sending a survey to AGM members on preferred location for this year's gala event

PRIORITIZE:

1. Book/secure venue at Banff Springs Hotel by end of day today
2. Send out calendar requests to all AGM members today
3. Review minutes from previous AGM meeting for any outstanding action items

ACTION:

1. Telephone Banff Springs: +1 403.123.1234
2. Telephone secretaries for AGM members; ensure next meeting is in calendars for March 15, 2003
3. Contact those who have not completed or executed the action items called for in the previous AGM meeting and obtain status report

Figure 14 – The PPA Method

My PPA system, as outlined in Figure 14, worked well because nothing fell through the cracks. A follow-through (or brought forward) system also worked wonders in ensuring that I stayed on top of things and doubled as a backup system. The jubilance I felt upon completion of a project or task using this methodology gave me a tremendous sense of accomplishment. No doubt, the list expanded daily as more responsibilities were inevitably added, but that is the nature of the job. The list never quite dwindles to nothing, and such an occurrence in today's market represents a threat to your position, in any case.

> *Plan*: Plan what work you will tackle for the day, week, month and year wherever possible. Planning consists of envisioning the task, job, or event well ahead of the due date. It should also consist of a thorough review of any meeting or event and the requisites for its

success. Planning should be combined with meticulous organization – the two readily go hand in hand. Aim to organize your time in tandem with the organization of your boss's time.

The ability to function in the midst of clutter is a rarity but not unheard of in the secretarial world. Some secretaries continue in this fashion unabated and perform their functions quite well. If your ability to plan effectively can only be fulfilled in a cluttered milieu, so be it. However, be aware that this may not always be acceptable for some bosses or organizations. If your boss is a neat freak, a constant mess on your desk or work space could ruin your relationship, and ultimately this could hold you back professionally. A time-management course can be beneficial in reducing or eliminating the tendency to accumulate clutter.

Prioritize: Upon completion of a thorough review and mental visualization of the desired goal, prioritize your work according to the timelines given for completing the project. The ability to prioritize is crucial for a secretary. Without it you will never be effective and are will be to struggle when crises arise. The opposite of prioritization is procrastination and complete disorganization. Shuffling can come into play, a process of repetitive and mindless shuffling of paper in a state of confusion and bewilderment. I learned early on the importance of prioritizing my work and how that translated into efficiency and a smooth workflow. I endeavoured never to jump into doing another unplanned task without completing the current one and following my specific, laid-out plan, except in cases of emergency or shifting priorities where my adaptability could be called into question. This occurred from time to time in my career, and in order to deal with sudden interruptions and changes, I adjusted my PPA plan or work schedule accordingly. Rigidity and a non-collaborative work style can serve as your downfall. Flexibility in accommodating unexpected situations is paramount, as well as the ability

> to comprehend and classify priorities and lay out the appropriate action plan.
>
> *Action*: The execution of tasks requires precision and decisiveness. Beyond that, in my experience, the two prior actions of planning and prioritizing made everything easier to manage, so I highly recommend instituting something similar to the PPA method for your daily routine. Once a task is complete, move on!

The PPA method enabled me to deal with shifting priorities with minimal angst. As you become more experienced, you will likely develop a system of your own that is equivalent to my PPA method, one that works for your personality and work environment. Microsoft Outlook provides excellent tools for managing your time and prioritizing your work. There are features to help you manage your tasks and keep an online journal, and you have the capability to flag your e-mails by order of importance and to assign a due date. Whatever method you choose, ensure you have a functional process in place for executing special projects in tandem with your daily tasks and tight deadlines, or you will overwhelm yourself unnecessarily.

The example below highlights the significance of multitasking and the right attitude for unflinchingly incorporating shifting priorities into your routine. It is taken from a real life situation.

> As soon as Sylvia walked into the office, the telephone on her desk was ringing. She took off her coat with one hand and reached for the ringing telephone with the other. It was her boss on the phone. He asked her to make two copies of page 5 of a report he had left on her desk and send one copy to the lawyers and the other to a client. Sylvia hung up the phone and her coat. She took the report off the desk and walked over to the photocopying machine. She turned on the photocopier, and while it was warming up she ran to the kitchen and made herself a cup of coffee. While at the coffee station, another executive approached her and asked if she wouldn't mind picking up some paperwork

from Accounts Payable and bringing it to him in the boardroom he was headed for. Sylvia fulfilled this request quickly, and upon her return to the photocopier it was warmed up and ready to go. She made the necessary copies and followed the instructions provided by her boss over the telephone. Many more tasks of this nature were fired at Sylvia on a daily basis, sometimes at the last moment, but she remained poised and completed each task in record time. Sylvia knew how to manage and maximize her time and how to complete the tasks laid out for her. Although it is apparent that multitasking is a breeze for her, the skill manifested itself as a result of years of experience.

Preparation of Documents

1. Take responsibility for the proper spelling of names and correct addresses when typing correspondence. When dictation refers to a specific document, look at the document for spelling, capitalization, formatting, and so on. If you are still uncertain, check the file for previous correspondence, or call the addressee's office and seek clarification from the receptionist or secretary.
2. If a memo or letter states that there are certain enclosures included with the correspondence, it is your responsibility to ensure that they are present.
3. Ensure that you thoroughly proofread everything that you type, concentrating on accuracy rather than speed.
4. All documents must follow the company's preferred writing style and corporate guidelines:
    a. If templates are available, use them; the communication experts in the company have spent a lot of time devising these templates to suit the corporate image.
    b. Take care to use the company name appropriately, protecting its trademark.

c. Never use the passive voice when writing business documents – the active voice is much more palatable and direct. Consider taking a business writing course with your local community college or online. In business, secretaries can be called upon to write or format business documents such as proposals, minutes of meetings, and reports, to name a few. A business writing course will help you organize your thoughts, write or type documents in the appropriate format and business language. Some employers will be happy to sponsor you as part of your career development.

d. Avoid technical jargon and acronyms that clients are not likely to understand.

e. Understand the difference between "customers" and "clients." Unless you work in retail, in the business market you are dealing with clients.

f. Do not over-sell your company or denigrate the competition; this is a turnoff for your clients.

5. Do not be afraid to request clarification from the author of the document you are typing if something does not read right or make sense; such questions will be appreciated.
6. Quite often you will be asked to print out a variety of complex documents for your boss. It is your responsibility to format the documents so that they print in a presentable format.
7. When using Microsoft Excel, it is your responsibility to ensure that the formulas, formatting, and hyperlinks within a spreadsheet function properly. If there are broken formulas or hyperlinks within the document, fix them. There is no need for your boss to know about the formula and formatting issues either. He just needs to be provided with a presentable, professional document and doesn't really care about the methods you use to achieve the task.

8. Date stamp all incoming letters, faxes, invoices, or other important documents and take the initiative to place copies on file.
9. Remember, anything you can do to reduce your boss's workload will be appreciated.

Arranging Meetings and Events

Booking meetings, meeting rooms, and event planning is another essential element in the secretary's job description. The meticulous organization called for in travel planning similarly applies to meeting and event planning. Secretaries working for high-powered executives are required to take the lead when planning both. Some of the activities associated with meeting planning include the following:

1. Organizing monthly and quarterly meetings
2. Taking the lead in maintaining department or company meeting diaries and arranging the meetings as requested
3. Soliciting openings in the schedules of the key stakeholders and guests invited to the meetings by coordinating with various departments and secretaries
4. Making appropriate travel and accommodation arrangements for out-of-town guests and attendees
5. Coordinating all the meeting and event logistics, such as the booking of conference rooms and transportation
6. Arranging refreshments and all the necessary catering requirements
7. Conducting research, compiling data, populating spreadsheets, and drafting outlines for consideration and presentation
8. Preparing and proofreading final materials and associated documents such as agendas, reports, and presentation documents for the meeting
9. Attending meetings if required to act as scribe
10. Accurately recording minutes of meetings and distributing to all interested parties

11. Taking the initiative to flag and follow up on action items arising from the meetings in a timely manner
12. Attending to the logistics after the meeting and ensuring that meeting facilities are left in the manner in which they were found
13. Developing guest lists for conferences, receptions, and other promotional activities and events

Meeting Notice Etiquette

Here are some guidelines to be followed when preparing and sending out meeting notices.

- If the meeting invitation is being sent to a senior executive or another VIP, the correct etiquette is to collaborate with his secretary and send e-mails, letters, and requests through her.
- Keep meeting notices short and sweet. Avoid long message bodies – these belong in the minutes of meetings.
- If you must attach meeting minutes or other documents to your invite, then place them in a network drive and provide a link to the participants. A central file location is also ideal because it protects proprietary information.
- Scheduling conflicts are inevitable, so be helpful and provide an update for each meeting time change so that participants understand the reason for the change.

Event Planning for Success

Large organizations will typically have a dedicated department for event planning. When those who are specialists in this field are planning an event for your group, they will do so in consultation with the head secretary. The logistical requirements fall within their purview, but they will consult you on style, timelines, locations, gift bags, overall cost, and several other items. Event planners are your friends and should be treated as such, because without them the responsibility falls on you.

Some organizations choose to outsource their event planning needs to an event management firm, or they will subcontract an individual to handle events on their behalf. Again, the event planner will work in concert with the senior secretary at the organization to complete the task.

For smaller firms with neither the budget nor the inclination to use outside help, event planning falls within the secretary's purview. To plan and execute a successful event, you simply need to follow these guidelines:

1. *Establish dates and times*

To be successful, you need to plan well in advance of the event date.

2. *Determine the budget*

Before you do anything else, you must know what funds you have at your disposal. Determine the budget for the entire enterprise. You cannot do any planning if you don't know how much you can spend.

3. *Secure the location*

As soon as you know the dates and the budget, you must now find and secure a location that is within your budget. Quite often this involves paying a deposit. Most secretaries are afforded corporate credit cards, so ensure you have enough credit to cover all eventualities.

4. *Book the caterer*

Depending on the type of event and where it is being held, you may need to find an independent company to cater it. Some venues will have an in-house event marketing representative who will take care of all these nuances for you. If the venue provides this organizer, it is important to check in with this person regularly to ensure that they understand your vision for the event. Clarify what they will and won't do for you. For instance, if you are planning an off-site team-building event, they may take care of booking hotel rooms, meeting rooms, refreshments, and other on-site logistics only. You may need to find a team-building coach yourself and ensure that his own requirements and vision for the event are realized.

5. *Send out the invitations*

In conjunction with points 1 to 4 above, you must send out the invitations for the event as quickly as possible to help those invited to avoid calendar conflicts.

Provide all the pertinent details about the event to avoid confusion:

- What is the event?
- Why and where is it being held?
- Did you provide clear directions and maps?
- What time does the event begin and end?
- Do invitees need to bring or do anything prior to the event? For example, do they need to make their own hotel reservations, organize transportation, et cetera? A star secretary will cover every eventuality and address all these concerns before they are raised. Transportation, flights, and hotel rooms need to be researched and booked well in advance of the actual day.

6. *Confirmations*

- Closer to the date of the event, you must confirm attendance and check-in with all key personnel and organizers.
- Never assume that an event will run smoothly; you must have contingency plans in place in case things do not go as planned. Plan for all eventualities.
- Keep the invitees informed and updated about any changes in the plans.

7. *Pre-event checklist*

- Communications – do the key players know their roles?
- Did you confirm the attendance of all the speakers?
- Do you have a backup speaker available in case of an emergency?
- Is the backup person fully apprised of the schedule of events?
- Do not overlook the small details, because your guests will not. Make sure you have addressed and taken care of the
- Seating plan
- Table setting
- Menu (including a consideration of food allergies)
- Program of events for the invitees
- Master of ceremonies (MC)

8. *On-site coordination*

- Whether it is a board meeting, a team-building exercise, a golf tournament, a company holiday party, or whatever the case may be, you must provide your emergency contact information to all interested parties.
- For a successful outcome, you must be present on site to oversee all operations.
- Assign roles and responsibilities to key personnel who you trust to deliver results.
- Execute the event as if your reputation depends on it, because it does!

9. *Handouts, giveaways, or gifts*

- It is your responsibility to ensure that all the meeting or event materials, resources, and tools are available for the attendees.
- Gift bags, raffles, and giveaways add a nice touch.

10. *Post-event checklist*

- For the sake of your firm and reputation, it is crucial that you leave the premises exactly as you found them.
- Transportation of guests to and from the event should be seamless.
- Assign a senior executive or the MC to conclude the event, with the appropriate thanks given to all the contributors.
- Conduct your own post-event review with your team, and use the outcomes for planning future events.

Travel Planning

Depending on a secretary's manager and his portfolio, her role will include some travel planning. As far as the manager is concerned, the secretary must be able to expertly book and manage his travel plans and changes with minimal difficulty.

Strength of character bodes well for a secretary who manages extensive travel. Pay attention to the following advice in order to avoid travel disasters.

1. During the first few weeks on a new job, sit your boss down and clarify the following:

    a. Given the ability to choose, determine his preferred travel times.

b. Ascertain his preferred airlines for national and/or international travel.

c. Determine his preferred seating location on the plane.

d. Confirm the transportation requirements, such as rental vehicle, taxi, or chauffeur-driven limousine. If his choice is to rent a vehicle, clarify the preferred size and model.

e. Find out his hotels of choice and other inclinations, including room preference (facing south or north, executive or deluxe suite) bed size (double/queen/king size), smoking or non-smoking, special requests for room service, gym, and spa options.

f. Establish what his favourite foods and restaurants are.

g. Make note of all allergies.

2. Aim for accuracy and always get answers for any queries or uncertainties you may have. Do not be afraid to ask more than once, as this will soon be forgotten. However, if you mess up, it will not.
3. Do not leave everything to the travel agencies. You need to be the one in control, so double-check everything.
4. Be known for being painstakingly thorough rather than the opposite.

An executive once shared with me an unfortunate incident resulting from his junior secretary's inexperience in making hotel room reservations. Displaying a lack of common sense and foresight, the secretary booked a "standard" hotel room in a very busy hotel for her six-foot-tall boss. Unable to upgrade to a more suitable room for another week because the hotel was filled to capacity, he spent the time sleeping at an uncomfortable angle in order to avoid dangling his feet off the tiny bed. When the boss confronted this secretary with his dissatisfaction, he soon realized the issues he had dealt with had never even entered her mind. Naturally, as long as this secretary worked for him, this boss wasn't going to trust her judgement. Doubtless this was a good learning opportunity for the junior secretary and a blunder she would likely never repeat in her career.

Unexpected Duties

As a professional secretary, you must be prepared for just about anything to be thrown at you, especially when hired to support senior management. Once again, you must embrace your inner octopus. It is possible that your boss will have high expectations, some of which will include the provision of personal support services over and above normal office duties. This is a very old-fashioned attitude, and those bosses who are "old school" will expect this of their secretaries. However, in this post-feminist society it is crucial that this issue is discussed at the interview. If you are uncomfortable and unwilling to veer from the job description and attend to your boss's personal affairs, you would be wise to make this known prior to being hired. Similarly, the hiring manager should clarify his expectations at the interview. The nature and extent of the personal work that a secretary can be called upon to do varies according to the individual she works for and the history of his relationships with previous secretaries. If an executive expects his secretary to run personal errands for him and none of his previous secretaries have objected to this, he will naturally assume that an incoming candidate will follow suit.

There are secretaries just starting out who wonder whether shorthand is still relevant in the secretarial job function. While shorthand is no longer a major post-millennium requirement, it can be useful at times. Many secretaries attend high-powered meetings and are required to take accurate minutes. Some executives are uncomfortable with tape recorders in these meetings, and the secretary needs to obtain approval from everyone attending the meeting prior to using one. Shorthand becomes very useful in such a situation, if one chooses to learn it.

Summary

- To be effective, competent, respected, and successful in your secretarial career, you need understand all the unwritten rules in your work environment.
- Polish your telephone etiquette.
- Taking telephone messages is an integral function of your job, so take great care in relaying messages correctly.
- Observe voice mail and e-mail etiquette.
- Internet use in a work environment is not a right but a privilege that must not be abused.
- Respect the confidential nature of your role and the intellectual property of your employer.
- Establish a filing system that not only makes sense to you but that others can also understand in your absence.
- Manage your time wisely.
- Multitasking and organizational skills should be second nature to a secretary.
- Execute all events as if your reputation depends on it, because it does!
- When planning travel, ask as many questions as you need to.
- Take pride in your work, and ensure that everything leaving your desk with your name on it is accurate and professional.
- Be prepared to handle unexpected and unusual requests.

Chapter 8: Temporary Secretaries

Working as a Temp

As the name implies, temporary secretaries are short-term workers brought in to fill a void created by vacancy, illness, vacation, or personal leave, such as maternity leave or leaves of absence. They are affectionately and commonly referred to as "temps"; the television journalist and presenter Evan Davis even described them on his BBC Radio 4 program *The Bottom Line* as "the employment equivalent of the one night stand."[25] While I had never heard of temporary employment referred to in this manner before, assignments can be as temporary as Davis's description suggests. However, I would argue, at least in this case, that both parties go into the arrangement knowing where they stand. There are no obligations on either side, and I concur with Davis's assessment that "it is a [mutual] short term relationship of convenience." It is possible to maintain a secretarial career primarily as a temp, depending on the economic climate of the city, country or area where one is based. While living in the UK in the 1990s, I chose to work as a temp in central London for approximately one year and was never unemployed. I even made assignment selections based on my interests, due to the wide choice of work opportunities available in London at the time.

The primary method of securing temporary work is through an employment agency. Rarely do employers advertise for temporary work using other channels. If they do, it is usually referred to as hiring someone "on contract," as "term employment," or as a "consultant," and

25 Evan Davis, *The Bottom Line*, BBC Radio 4, June 23, 2011, http://www.bbc.co.uk/programmes/b01206c6.

the contract usually lasts from six months to a year. Secretaries hired in this manner are known as "contractors."

Employment agencies act as middlemen, assessing the candidates on behalf of their clients. They typically maintain a roster of temps that they rely upon for emergency placements but are constantly on the lookout for fresh talent. Prior to adding a candidate to their books, employment agencies will carry out rigorous tests for the appropriate skills such as word processing and typing speed, and conduct a reference check. They then carefully match the candidate's test results and credentials to the criteria presented by their clients.

In order to match the right candidate with the right client and vice versa, agencies will sometimes visit their clients' premises to assess the company's culture and environment. They make it their business (or at least they should) to learn all that they can about the company's history, its internal and external reputation, vision, mission statement, level of employee satisfaction, benefits structure, annual turnover, dress code, opportunities for growth, and anything else they think the temp might need to know. This information comes in handy particularly when a temporary assignment converts into a permanent job offer.

The highly publicized and devastating recession that hit the world economy in 2008 highlighted the need for temporary workers and opened up this avenue to those who never considered that they could be candidates for temporary status with any employer. In conversing with some of my friends who work as secretaries, their chief complaints about their work life during this tumultuous period were consistent:

1. Employers were engaging in numerous layoffs, which placed a huge workload burden on the permanent employees.
2. Some employees were working longer (unpaid) hours to justify or leverage their job security.
3. Morale was low.
4. The work environment had grown more competitive.

Why would any employer resort to hiring temporary workers? Quite possibly for any one of the following economically biased reasons:

1. They do not need to pay any benefits to temporary workers. This not only means no health coverage but also none of the ancillary benefits that come with being a full-time employee, such as RRSP matching, company cell phones, paid time off, or any of the perks that regular employees enjoy.
2. They can limit employment contracts by hiring staff only when the company needs them.
3. They can be selective with temporary staff by picking the best of the crop for a modest pay rate.

Temporary secretaries must be extremely reliable and trustworthy, or they will find it difficult to obtain work. Unreliable temps quickly fall off the agencies' books. More importantly, temps must possess certain characteristics and have a particular personality and skill in order to be successful and secure future assignments. That special breed is an individual who demonstrates the following characteristics:

- Adaptable
- Able to switch gears easily from one organizational culture to another.
- Able to adapt to working for and with different personalities.
- Able to learn new systems and processes quickly and easily, without fuss.
- Unflappable
- Takes criticism well and does not get easily offended
- Brings a sense of maturity to the job
- Behaves in a professional and mature manner
- Approachable
- Must be likeable and friendly in order to fit in.
- Must embody openness, a "willing and able to help" attitude, and a demeanour that endears others to you and makes them feel comfortable about asking you for assistance.

Some companies prefer to "test drive" secretaries by hiring them initially as temps and then dangle the carrot of full-time employment in front of them if certain conditions are met. These conditions are generally the same as those highlighted in chapter 3 of this book about interviews. The candidate must be a good fit, must be able to handle the job at hand, and must be a consummate professional. Some companies will highlight such intentions up front, while others will surreptitiously hire a temp without divulging their true intention.

Employers have every right to hire secretaries on a "temp to perm" basis. The hiring process can be arduous and costly. It is the employer's prerogative to choose wisely. This in no way reflects negatively on the temp. Generally if a position is high profile, political, demanding, or has security sensitivities, then the employer would rather err on the side of caution, particularly if there have been problems with prior incumbents. If you are hired on a "temp to permanent" basis, you should consider yourself lucky because you are essentially a free agent who can leave the situation at any time if it proves unsuitable. At the same time, you can prove yourself to be the right candidate for the role and combine your probationary period and temporary opportunity to your advantage. Such a situation is a win-win for both sides. The employer has the chance to be sure that you are the right fit while you can also appraise the role and employer for suitability according to your own benchmarks.

It is my experience that when a full-time secretary is made redundant or laid off from a permanent job, she need not fret because she can immediately pivot to working as a temp. The beauty of being a qualified secretary is the fact that opportunities are nearly always available and secretaries are rarely out of work for long. If they cannot find the ideal permanent position, there is always temping. Even those secretaries who are terminated with cause or fired can immediately switch over to temporary secretarial work, as long as they can get someone to vouch for their work ethic and provide them with good references.

Temping is an excellent way of acquiring varied work experience. In fact, some secretaries use temping as a stepping-stone towards full-time employment, or as a way to get their foot in the door of companies that they have a high regard for and would like to join – all perfectly acceptable strategies for finding gainful employment.

As I have already mentioned, in order to match the right candidate with the right client and vice versa, employment agencies will sometimes visit their clients' premises to assess the culture and environment. However, when a permanent job offer is presented, it is always prudent for a temp to conduct her own research into the potential employer prior to accepting the offer, as opposed to relying on the agency's findings. Sometimes an agency is remiss in conducting their research, so be sure that you're as well informed as you can be.

This practice came in handy for me in my career, when one employment agency arranged a job interview for me for a position that was billed as "temp to permanent." The job was that of executive assistant to the company's president and CEO. Part of the role involved the management of the president's personal and business affairs, biweekly travel, and some minimal assistance to his wife.

In an attempt to fully prepare myself for the interview and impress a potential employer with my knowledge of his business empire, I went on the Internet and Googled this entrepreneur's name, and I was taken aback by what I found out about him. There, in black and white, were newspaper reports outlining accusations of sexual harassment and corruption levelled against him by previous employees and business associates. In confronting the employment agency with these findings, I learned that they were aware of these allegations and had discussed them with the client, who had explained them away in a sufficiently satisfactory manner for the agency to continue working with him. However, the allegations against this potential employer were disturbing to me, and media coverage of some of his insalubrious business practices lit up a warning light in my head. This wasn't going to be the right environment for me.

In my capacity as an office manager some years ago, I contacted an employment agency and asked them to send me an experienced filing clerk for a special project that would last approximately three months. They sent me someone they billed as a "filing wiz," and upon meeting her I felt comfortable that she could do the job. The first two months of her contract, she excelled. However, as the third month approached, certain negative characteristics in her work ethic began to show. She consistently arrived late for work, spent long periods of time on the telephone on personal calls, and would sneak out early when she thought that no one was observing. This was very disappointing to me, as I had been considering extending her contract. This is a prime example of why employers would rather test drive a temporary secretary before hiring one on a permanent basis. Experience has taught me that people will indeed show you their true colours when they become comfortable in their environment, and this is usually after the probationary period has passed. In fact, some employers are aware of this human trait and would rather hire contractors for a defined trial period, such as a six- or twelve-month contract, before converting them to permanent employees. I must say that although this may appear to be a disadvantage for the hardworking, dedicated temp, it is beneficial for the employer in the long run and perfectly reasonable.

Of course, the reverse is also true. Some employers are quite capable of misrepresenting themselves to the employee. As a temp in one particular situation, I did observe something unpleasant about my temporary employment status. I accepted a short-term assignment working in a role that I considered somewhat junior to the types of positions I was used to. Temping was preferable at that point in my life for various personal reasons. Although the employment agency that placed me had made me fully aware of the somewhat unappealing history of the role, the manager's confrontational style, and his difficulties in trying to hire a suitable secretary to complement his working style, I decided to go into the position with an open mind, and accepted the assignment. While engaged in this role as a temp, my boss seemed courteous, accommodating, and respectful in his behaviour towards me, and at first I did not see any evidence of the aforementioned antagonistic management style in the way he conversed with me. Six months into my assignment, this manager realized that he had a very experienced, efficient, and hard-working secretary in his employ, so he approached me about converting to a "term employee" on a twelve-month direct contract with the company as opposed to working via the employment agency. I considered the offer and decided to accept it, and only then did the manager's style and personality change for the worse. The courteous and respectful mannerisms slowly disappeared, and he morphed into a condescending, narcissistic micro-manager. As his behaviour worsened, I realized there was no way that I would last working in this environment for twelve months, much less endure his nonsensical behaviour, so I quit five months into the new contract.

I later learned that the assistant preceding me had suffered the same ridicule as I had. Clearly, anyone walking into the role of supporting this manager would be unaware of the Jekyll and Hyde personality of her boss until she was hired for a longer-term contract. In reading this unpleasant tale, you might well ask about the role of the human resources advisor (HRA) in this fiasco and wonder why an employee must endure such behaviour. This is another disadvantage of being a temporary worker or contractor. Indeed, the employee has rights, but office politics come into play here. Naturally, the HRA might smooth things over with you and assure you that he or she will investigate the matter and advocate for you, but in truth, when you blow the whistle, it won't be long before the consequences arise. In this scenario, it is likely that the employment agency that placed you will be contacted and advised that "you are not working out," at which point you will be replaced. When engaged as a direct contractor to the company, it is more than likely that the HRA will endeavour to mediate to work things out between you and your boss, but in reality the relationship is tainted, and the trust and respect on either side are gone. How long a secretary decides to stay in this environment is entirely up to her, but if the boss decides he no longer wants you working for him, you will be terminated for some imaginative reason, and there is really not much you can do about it if you want to keep working and secure other lucrative jobs. I have seen a few instances where employees have brought an unjust dismissal case against the employer, but these can be long and drawn out, and because these roles are not usually unionized, it is an unnecessary headache for you unless you have the appetite to engage in a losing battle against a past employer with deep pockets.

The examples given here for either side are somewhat extreme; in earnest, most temporary jobs are fun and run their course without incident. The reader is asked to note that the downside of temporary working status as described in this chapter is presented *only as a precaution.*

Temporary assignments can be open-ended for many reasons, based on the employer's ultimate goal for the role. Secretaries who are temping because they are in between jobs and are on the hunt for full-time employment need to approach temp work with great caution and must have a clear understanding with the employer about the duration of their assignment as well as their own goals. If a secretary is temping because she has lost her own permanent position for whatever reason, it is imperative that she let it be known to prospective temporary employers that she is actively looking for work and will be attending interviews while working for them. Furthermore, the temporary secretary should also make it clear to the employer that should she land a permanent job while temping for them, she will give them a certain amount of notice and then expect to quit her temporary role for the permanent opportunity. The employer and the temporary worker are dealing with "unknowns" in this case, and it is crucial that both parties understand this. Not clarifying these realities from the outset can create resentment. Furthermore, it may result in an ungraceful exit for the temp, should she find herself in a position where she has a permanent job offer but is stuck in a temporary job in which her employer is assuming that she will act as an indefinite stopgap.

Working as a temp requires the temporary worker to be loyal only to herself at times because the employment agency and the temporary employer are quite often only concerned about their own needs. While they understand the temp's predicament, they will feel somewhat maligned if she decides to leave them suddenly because she has landed herself a permanent position with another firm. One senior secretary I know was in a contract position for twelve months, covering a leave of absence for an employee who was travelling abroad with every intention of returning to her role at the end of the time period. Six months into that contract, the temporary secretary landed a permanent position with another company and broke her contract with the employer and the employment agency that had placed her in that role. From her perspective, the permanent position was an incredible opportunity which she believed was the right fit for her. She felt she had no option but to take it despite the repercussions it would have on her immediate situation. In the agency's and the employer's eyes, she had left the company in the lurch, which meant they had to scramble to find someone else to complete those remaining six months. This put her at odds with the employment agency and the company, but it is the nature of the business.

While writing this book, I reflected a great deal on my temp days back in London, England, and recalled that I once accepted a temporary position with a verbal and very loosely defined "six-month" agreement. Towards the end of the of the six months, I suddenly found myself at odds with the employment agency and the temporary employer when I announced that my time was up and I was leaving to take another position. The employment agency and the employer had simply assumed that I would just sit there indefinitely and wait for them to make a decision when it suited them. They had paid no attention to the time that had elapsed, so I reminded them a week prior that my time was coming to an end. They responded by imploring me to stay on another couple of months. Indeed, I could have extended my contract indefinitely if I had enjoyed the assignment, or if the employer made it an attractive place for me to want to work and the company executive I was supporting treated me fairly, with dignity and respect. However, this was not the case, and I had better plans. An employer I had worked for previously was beckoning me to return for an opportunity that might eventually lead to full-time employment, and given that he had treated me fairly and with appreciation and that it was a great place to work, I was inclined to accept his proposal. From my perspective, I had fulfilled my six-month commitment to my present employer. I was now a free agent and was moving on to another opportunity that I had secured on my own, without the agency's assistance. Needless to say, the employer was far from pleased that I wasn't putting his company's needs first, and the employment agency dropped me from their books permanently! Again, I highlight this scenario to make other secretaries aware of the advantages and disadvantages of working as a temp.

It is also possible for the temporary secretary to come into a temporary role, possibly covering for vacation, maternity, sick or personal leave, and actually pose a threat to the permanent employee. Although employment standards and the labour codes protect the permanent employee from being replaced by the temporary secretary, however excellent she might be, things can still bode well for the temporary secretary. Should circumstances change and the position open up in the future, employers, if they so choose, can make a special request via the employment agency that the temporary secretary who so impressed them return for future coverage or consideration for a permanent situation.

On the whole, as with any job, a secretary's temporary status should not dictate how she conducts herself professionally. The world is indeed a small place, and a colleague can turn out to be a future boss or influence a future position; people do move around and can turn up on an interviewing panel for a future position that you are eager to get. If you are fond of a particular industry, mergers and acquisitions can bring the most unlikely firms together, resulting in a previous employer suddenly becoming your new employer. Your prior conduct can therefore affect whether you are hired in another position or are promoted to a senior role, so all temporary secretaries would do well to bear this in mind as they navigate the temporary job circuit.

Advantages and Disadvantages

Advantages

1. You will obtain unique, varied, and interesting experience acquired as a result of working in wide-ranging industries and organizations.
2. You can choose assignments and working hours.
3. You cannot be drawn into the politics of any particular organization.

4. It's a great way to observe and decide on a chosen industry or area of specialization.
5. It's a fantastic way to get your foot in the door and learn about an organization's structure and culture.
6. Hourly rates of compensation can be much higher for temps than they would be if employed on a full-time basis.
7. You'll have the opportunity to network and make many friends in the various companies that you temp for.
8. You'll have the luxury of accepting or denying a job offer without repercussions or regret, especially in a vibrant economy.
9. Any hours you work over and above the contracted hours are paid at an agreed overtime rate, and sometimes if you work over a certain weekly threshold, your employment agency can request time and a half or more.
10. Holidays are at your discretion; you can take time off whenever you want. The onus is on the employment agency to provide cover or a substitute.

Disadvantages

1. It may be difficult to secure full-time employment if your employment history is primarily that of being a temp. Some employers are wary about temps and prefer secretaries who have solid, quantifiable, related experience.
2. There are a lack of benefits that come with permanent employment, such as bonuses, stock options, and health coverage.
3. Temporary workers must be aware that they could be treated as an outsider. Some employers may deliberately exclude a temp from attending company events or from being privy to sensitive company information.
4. Sick days and holidays are not compensated. You are paid by the hour from the time you show up to the time you leave.
5. Depending on where you live, the associated federal laws, and the agency's policy, you may not get paid for statutory holidays and vacations where full-time employees do.

6. Employment agencies may charge their clients (your temporary employer) an exorbitant hourly rate for your services but only pay you a fraction of the amount. In fact, some agencies will expressly state in their rules of engagement that the temp must refrain from discussing her hourly wage with the client or other temporary staff. For example, the agency could charge the client $45 per hour but pay you $30 per hour. The difference of $15 covers the agency's costs for finding you the job, conducting tests to ensure you meet the client's criteria, placing you, and of course paying you up front for your services. Furthermore, the agency is on the hook for providing a replacement should you prove unsuitable, and there are risks and costs associated with this endeavour.
7. Sometimes assignments are extremely short and you miss out on establishing great friendships.
8. If a company doesn't take to you, they reserve the right to refuse to hire you in the future, which may affect your prospects.
9. Temporary workers are expected to come into an assignment and adapt immediately to their environment and the task at hand.
10. Most companies view temps as experts in their field, and therefore the expectations are very high and the learning curve afforded is minimal.
11. Temps will often be assigned the jobs that no one in the organization wants to do.
12. Dry periods can lead to anxiety; you may not be able to find work all year round.
13. Employment agencies can become possessive of their temps, expecting them to work for no other agency but theirs, which can lead to dry periods and loss of income. In fact, when some agencies learn that you are not working exclusively for them, they simply stop calling you.
14. Temporary work is not guaranteed, and the income potential is unreliable; contracts can be terminated at any time at the discretion of the employer.

15. Upon signing you on as a temporary employee, employment agencies will give you their own behavioural guidelines, which you must follow as long as you are on an assignment that represents the agency.

Temping Guidelines

1. *Be on time*

Punctuality is a huge priority for temps. If you can't avoid being late, you must call the employment agency at least an hour to an hour and a half prior to your scheduled start time. This is not only courteous but also gives the agency the time to notify the client that you will be late. The same applies if you must be absent for any reason.

Do not call ten minutes before your start time; be considerate and give the agency the chance to find a replacement for you if you are unable to fulfil your assignment on a particular day.

2. *Be professional*

People often use this word loosely, but in this case it refers to your conduct: being courteous, considerate, discreet, and respectful. Do not take extended lunches at will. If you must leave the assignment to attend another job interview or medical appointment, contact the agency and inform them of your intentions. Avoid disappearing acts.

Never abuse the client's resources, such as computers, faxes, printers, and telephones. If you want to make a personal call, use your own cell phone during your lunch break. If you must use the client's telephone in an emergency, inform your assigned supervisor first and then be as brief as possible.

Refrain from giving out the client's number to your friends as a means of contacting you, as this is unacceptable and unprofessional behaviour.

3. *Be confidential*

When a company opens its doors to you and allows you into its fold, it does so with the expectation that you will conduct yourself with the utmost integrity and professionalism and that any and all information shared with you will go no further. If you cannot be trusted, you really have no business being a temp or a secretary of any kind. Discretion equals secretary.

4. *Clarify goals and timelines*

Be sure that everyone understands your goals and intentions if you are actively searching for other employment. Let people know how this could impact your current assignment and have the agency and employer clarify for you exactly how long your assignment is and when it ends so there are no illusions or misunderstandings about timelines.

5. *Recognize opportunities*

Never approach the temporary employer and canvass for a permanent position or beg for a job. However, if they approach you in this regard, immediately refer them to your agency. The agency will do all the negotiations necessary on your behalf.

6. *Avoid gossip*

Refrain from engaging in office gossip. If other people are chitchatting around you, do not join in. The client pays you an hourly wage and expects you to fulfil your duties in the allotted time.

7. *Don't get too comfy*

Rearranging furniture is not wise, particularly if you are covering for someone who is away on vacation. If you must adjust a chair or a computer monitor to be comfortable that's fine, but be sure to put them back in their original settings when your assignment is over. The incumbent should return to a desk and furniture arrangement that looks exactly as she left them.

Do not put up personal posters or change screen savers on the computer; this is not your property.

Never loan or borrow anything from the client's office or from their staff.

Refrain from sending personal e-mails from the client's office or providing the client's e-mail account as your personal contact info.

Do not read magazines, books, or play computer games while at the client site, even if it is after the core hours of work.

8. *Avoid flirting*

Inappropriate behaviour such as flirting with office staff, consuming alcohol, or engaging in office romances is unprofessional, unwise, and will undoubtedly lead to immediate termination.

Avoid discussing your personal life with anyone at the client office.

9. *Beware of personality conflicts*

Any personality conflicts that adversely affect your work should be reported to the agency. They will remove you from the situation immediately and arrange for a replacement.

10. *Avoid office politics*

There is a tendency on the part of some clients to blame temporary staff for anything that goes wrong or missing within the office. Counter such baseless accusations by bringing the bare minimum to the client's property in a small handbag. You should always be transparent and never remove items that don't belong to you from the client's place of business.

11. *Get your time sheet signed*

At the end of each assignment, temps must have a supervisor sign and approve their time sheets. In the first instance, before using the client's fax machine to send your time sheet to the agency, obtain permission to do so from the supervisor. However, most agencies have progressed with the technological times and are using web-based time sheets, which give employees the ability to submit hours to their manager electronically, resulting in the manager approving the time sheet instantly, with no lag time. The drawback with this process is that if the manager doesn't log in to his computer or e-mail to approve the time sheet, the process is stalled. The onus is on the employee to have the time sheet approved.

There are many rules affecting temporary secretaries. However, these depend on the client's flexibility towards temporary staff. Ideally, the same rules should be transferred to permanent situations, but common sense is usually a good guide for the novice temporary secretary.

A select number of secretaries prefer temping to full-time employment and enjoy the unpredictability of their chosen assignments, the variety of the work and the opportunity to meet different people in a work environment. Looking back on my own experiences, I enjoyed my time as a temporary secretary immensely, and in some cases I learned a great deal more than I would have working in a permanent position with just one company. The varied experiences I had stood me in very good stead for future experiences.

Summary

- When the economic climate is healthy, it is quite possible to maintain a secretarial career primarily as a temp.
- Temporary assignments are generally acquired via an employment agency. Rarely do employers advertise for temporary secretarial opportunities.
- Be prepared to undergo rigorous testing if you sign up for temporary work with an employment agency, and be aware that signing on with too many agencies can in fact work against you.
- As an employee of the agency, you must adhere to the agency's own employment guidelines.
- Temping is a good stepping-stone for an inexperienced secretary while also offering flexibility to the experienced secretary who chooses to work in temporary assignments instead of full-time positions.
- There are advantages and disadvantages that must be considered if one chooses to work solely as a temp.
- Clarify timelines, assignment length, and your employer's goals, and ensure that your own intentions are known to everyone involved to avoid confusion and conflict.
- Try your best to make a graceful exit from your temporary employer. If you are in the wrong assignment, it is better to speak up and leave as gracefully as possible than to perpetuate a bad situation.

- When an offer of full-time, permanent employment is presented to you, conduct thorough research on the potential employer to avoid surprises to ensure that the opportunity is everything you're hoping for.

Chapter 9:
The Boss(es)

Working for One Boss

The relationship between a secretary and her boss is a delicate dance where the two play off one another's sensitivities. It is a give-and-take type of relationship, a union, and as such I like to compare it to a marriage. There are many similarities, but with two exceptions: the exclusion of the more personal intimacy that exists in a real marriage and the fact that there is one dominant party. Both parties learn to work and cohabitate with each other through the defined work week, and considering the fair portion of time that is spent at the office by most workers, synchronicity in this type of relationship is crucial.

The boss and his secretary must interact almost daily to compare notes and match calendars and also to discuss departmental issues, upcoming events, travel requirements, meetings, and myriad projects. The secretary often plays the role of gatekeeper, which translates into managing the boss's time, appointments, and travel. She must stay apprised of all of her boss's movements and should always be in a position to pinpoint his whereabouts in moments of crisis. Even the boss's wife may have to consult the secretary about her husband's schedule.

With few exceptions, internal and external clients cannot and should not bypass the secretary or assistant in order to arrange a meeting with the boss. A seasoned executive will refer those individuals back to his secretary to keep the process consistent and lend some semblance of respect to her role. However, some managers and executives, particularly higher-level managers, will deliberately go over the secretary's head. The reason for this kind of behaviour is typically arrogance and/or disrespect for the secretary. The prescription for dealing with such unsavoury personalities was covered in chapter 4 of this book.

The extent to which the secretary's role is considered important is dependent on her boss's view. Some have been known to describe their secretaries as their right hand. When this is said of you, take it as a compliment because it means you are doing your job well and the relationship is working.

Quite often a secretary will regularly interact with the boss's family and close friends, and it is also feasible for her to cultivate a close friendship with his wife. If there is an agreement at the beginning that some of your responsibilities will include the management of your boss's personal affairs, then you should look upon his wife as your second boss. To be successful in your role, you need to adopt a collaborative approach to managing any personal matters that affect your two "bosses." However, if there is a clear understanding at the outset that your job description does not include anything that pertains to your boss's personal life, then his wife cannot and should not be encouraged to order you about. Your one and only boss is the one who writes your paycheck. Even then, as a secretary, you will make your job that much easier if you do all that you can to get on with the boss's wife. On those rare occasions when you do get dubious requests that are outside of your agreed job description, convey your unease to your boss in a courteous manner.

I once attended an interview for a position that called for serving two masters – a husband-and-wife team. Halfway through the interview, I started to have reservations about whether this was a position for which I would be a good fit, or indeed where I could even be successful. During the interview, the two argued incessantly in front of me and would cut each other off as they each tried to drive a point home. I was extremely uncomfortable throughout the interview and foresaw major problems managing the two of them. After the interview, I withdrew myself from the running.

When you are hired on as a secretary, your primary role is to make your boss's work life easier. Your boss doesn't need to know exactly how you go about doing so, and neither does anyone else. In most cases, the boss is not interested and quite possibly doesn't care how you excel in your job. All that matters to him is that you are doing it well. In other words, you should avoid bragging or seeking glory for the minor fires that you put out on his behalf. Not only is this an immature way to behave, but it really isn't necessary, because the fewer problems there are, the more indispensable you are. The only way to gauge whether your competency and extra efforts are appreciated by your boss is during your absence from the office. For instance, while you are away on vacation, someone will need to cover your position and maintain the same superior level of service and astuteness. Should the stand-in fail to do so, your boss will be chewing his nails off by the time you return. He will most likely be apprehensive about your future vacations, and this is high praise indeed!

When your boss becomes too reliant on you this can be flattering, but there is a downside. He becomes possessive about you, and it becomes increasingly difficult to get anyone to step into your shoes during your absence. Nonetheless, secretaries whose bosses value them as highly as this generally enjoy their work and tend to stay in the same position for their entire career because of the good working relationship. With tenure and an appreciative boss come extremely good pay and perks, and a seasoned secretary who understands how difficult it can be to find a really good position knows better than to leave it. Every secretary should strive for this level of success.

In an earlier chapter (Chapter 3: Interview Guidelines), I emphasized the importance of interviewing the prospective employer with as much vigour as they apply when interviewing you to ensure that it is the right situation for both sides. The major reason behind this tête-à-tête is to determine in your own mind if you can give positive responses to the following key questions:

1. Do I feel comfortable in the presence of this individual?

2. Do I feel as if this is someone I can come to respect and work very closely with every weekday?
3. Do I know all that I need to at this stage to help me decide whether to accept this position?
4. Do I want to work here? (For example, if you have questions you need answered, such as whether your role includes running personal errands or managing your boss's personal life, it's best to find this out sooner than later.)

If you have doubts, then you need to take some time to ponder whether this would be a good fit for both parties. It is unfair to accept the position and later decide to leave because your doubts have been confirmed. The hiring process is costly and time consuming for employers. When you find yourself having doubts immediately after an interview and your gut feeling is that the position may not be right for you for whatever reason, then the prospective employer has not impressed you and the right thing to do would be to pass on the opportunity and wait until the right situation presents itself. The relationship with your boss should be based on mutual respect in order for it to work. If it is, the guiding principles I am about to outline in this chapter will not be an issue for you.

Building Rapport

As you get to know your new boss, you may regularly engage in small talk in an effort to get to know each other. Tread carefully and know when to draw the line with small talk, and never overdo it. Let your boss set the tone for the conversation and overall relationship. If he goes beyond your comfort level with small talk, excuse yourself immediately and head back to work. He will soon get the message.

Avoid being too forward, using expletives, or any other behaviour that calls your professionalism into question. At the beginning, your boss may excuse any gaffes you make. However, if you continue to slip up, he will start to keep count. Any behaviour that is deemed unacceptable might be discussed immediately upon occurrence or postponed until a quarterly or annual performance review. These sessions should reinforce your important role in the company and the department in which you work. Ideally, the occasion should be an opportunity for your boss to tell you how invaluable you are and for you to seize the moment to discuss your professional development or request a raise or promotion. If, instead, you have scores of negative strikes against you, it may take a long time to repair your boss's trust, and other secretaries will be recognized ahead of you.

All of the above notwithstanding, I must note here that some unscrupulous bosses use the performance review as an opportunity to tell you everything that you are doing wrong or to complain about whatever habit you have that they do not like. He may not mention it throughout the year but will bring it up at this crucial time to counter any demands you make for a pay raise. Be aware of this fact and defend yourself in a non-confrontational manner. If any of the criticism is constructive, take it with humility and express your desire to do better, and ideally the matter will end there. Most executives will only criticize you because they want you to do better and do not want a repeat of the act that has caused them concern. If, however, the criticism is unfounded and is rather a personal attack from an unprincipled boss, do not retaliate. Instead, return to your work station and document the incident. If this persists, then we are dealing with an entirely different situation, and as you read on, my views on how to handle it will be clearer. In truth, if you really do work for someone like that, I suggest that you do one of two things:

1. Thank him for his remarks and then tell him that while you do not agree with his observation and review of your performance, you will accept it nonetheless and promise to do better.
2. Accept the criticism and concerns he brings forth with no argument, and then immediately begin your search for another position where your efforts will be appreciated.

It is essential that the chemistry between you and your boss be agreeable. Unlike a married couple, who can seek counselling or work on their issues, most secretaries are dispensable. If the relationship between you and your boss is not working, someone has to leave, and that someone is *you*. Life is too short to be unhappy at work, so if you need to, move on. If you decide to stick it out, remember to do all that is in your power to be viewed as close to indispensable as possible.

The type of boss who hires a secretary and then proceeds to minimize her role by not engaging her in high-level discussions or departmental initiatives because he just assumes that she possesses low-level intelligence and is incapable of rational and effective collaboration couldn't be more wrong. Executives or managers who operate in this manner are often not well versed in the effective use of their secretarial resource. This is a shame, because secretaries, given half the chance, partner up with their boss for the good of the company and can help him shine. However, at times an unscrupulous boss will flagrantly take credit for a secretary's idea (it happened to Melanie Griffith's character in the movie *Working Girl*). Moreover, a bad boss will quash this vital contribution if he does not treat his secretary with due respect. Secretaries take personal responsibility for resolving issues that benefit the company at large, even when the rewards for success will not necessarily accrue to them directly.

As a secretary, your role is vital not only where your immediate boss is concerned but for the rest of the organization. As a dedicated professional, it is important to nurture your relationship with your boss's staff by being a team player. It makes your life that much easier when you get on with the rest of your team. They are your allies and may pass on accolades directly to your boss about any outstanding efforts on your behalf. They will also defend you either from your boss or the rest of the organization. Like everything else in life, one or two people on the team may not see eye to eye with you, possibly due to a personality conflict or mutual dislike. This will happen occasionally throughout your career, and it is something you will have to learn to deal with using appropriate professionalism.

Making It Work

Effective Listening: Sharpen your Listening Skills

Usually when you start working for someone, the rules are laid out. Your boss will advise you how he likes to have his office run and outline his expectations. Ask as many questions as you can at the beginning to ensure that you know what those expectations are. A good thing to do at the outset is to go over the job description together with him to be sure that both sides understand what is on paper. Try not to second-guess yourself or your boss because it gets you nowhere, and neither will making assumptions. Listen carefully, and if you are uncertain, ask! The boss may appear annoyed at you for asking many questions, but this is only temporary because he ultimately wants you to get things right and would rather you ask than make numerous mistakes. Take notes as instructions are fired at you. The boss will indeed be annoyed if he has clarified something repeatedly yet you consistently forget and have to keep checking with him. Make good, comprehensive notes!

Set Goals and Standards of Working

Maintain your professionalism by setting realistic goals and standards for yourself, and be sure that you set standards that you can live up to. Goals give you something to aim for and provide a sense of meaning to your work. But do not commit to something that's beyond your capabilities only to falter. If you are having trouble meeting a deadline, you need to speak up about any issues you are having. Your boss is not psychic, so you need to keep him informed of your workload and advise him of any hiccups in the flow of your productivity.

When setting acceptable and unacceptable work standards for yourself, carefully examine your core values, and the task will be that much easier. Carrying out this small but important step sets the tone for the calibre of your work, your personality at work, your relationship with your peers and your boss, and most importantly your sense of self. I encourage you to do this exercise as soon as you are hired for a new secretarial position. Think about the kind of work you will be doing, the culture at that organization, the person you will be calling your boss, and the vision and business of the company. Then use the SMART method[26] of goal planning:

- **S**pecific – Set explicit and clearly defined goals that make sense to you, your boss, and the organization.
- **M**easurable – How do you know when you have reached your goal? Document your goals so that they are measurable and evidence-based.
- **A**ttainable – Are the goals realistic, or pie in the sky? Do not commit to something that you cannot deliver, as doing so affects your credibility and professional reputation.
- **R**elevant – Set goals that are relevant to your role as opposed to things it would be nice to have. Will your goals make a difference to you, your job, your boss, and the overall departmental and organizational goals?
- **T**imeline – What is the timeline for achieving these goals? Set realistic and achievable timelines for meeting them. What happens if you cannot meet a deadline? Consider whether your timelines are practical, sensible, and viable.

Rules of Engagement for the Elite Secretary

To be counted among the very best in the field largely depends on your conduct, integrity, and professionalism.

Personal conduct

- Be the very best secretary you can be in all facets of your work.
- Be self-directed, flexible, and adaptable.
- Use diplomacy and tact when resolving conflicts.
- Be assertive when required yet approachable and pleasant.
- Strive to make only a few mistakes (preferably none); own up and learn from the mistakes that you do make.
- Take ownership and be accountable.

---

26 Martin Kloess, "SMART Goals – A Key to Success," *Allvoices.com*, accessed June 25, 2011, http://allvoices.com/contributed-news/5507269-smart-goals-a-key-to-success.

- Be proactive. Try to solve problems/customer complaints yourself, or try to find a resolution to a problem instead of taking every small issue to the boss.

Integrity

- Keep your emotions in check.
- Keep your personal life private unless it is something that directly affects your work (e.g., having surgery, death in the family).
- Never, ever compromise your integrity or values.
- Never tolerate rudeness or attacks of a personal nature on any matter unrelated to your work.
- Do the right thing, even if it isn't the popular or politically correct thing to do.
- Always tell the truth, even if it will get you into trouble.

Professionalism

- Set the bar very high for yourself and all that you do in your professional capacity.
- Practice professional and ethical behaviour.
- Never bite the hand that feeds you by instigating malicious gossip or disclosing any information conveyed to you in confidence.
- Never take anything unpleasant that is said in the heat of the moment too personally – rather, try to understand the stresses of the corporate world.
- Maintain loyalty, trust, and confidentiality – the mainstays of a secretary's role.
- Have an exit strategy. Know when it is time to move on.

The Loyalty and Trust Factor

A secretary's loyalty is to her boss first and foremost and then to the organization she works for and its staff. It is unprofessional for a secretary to instigate malicious gossip or negative talk about her boss. As a secretary, you will be privy to a lot of personal and confidential material that you should never repeat to others in any shape or form.

Many years ago, on my very first job while attending secretarial school, I was hired as a part-time receptionist for an auto repair centre. Although my title was "receptionist," I was pseudo-secretary to the big boss – the president. His office was adjacent to the reception area, and he pretty much treated me like his personal secretary, which was good training for me. Soon after my first week on the job I began to notice something strange, but I couldn't confirm it with anyone or talk about it. I just sat at reception feeling puzzled. One of the female executives at this firm would go into the boss's office once or twice a day and shut the door behind her. Other managers never bothered to do so, and all major meetings took place in the boardroom. This lady or my boss always made a point of shutting the door when they entered his office. Their meetings behind the closed door would invariably go on for two hours at a minimum, leaving me dumbfounded. Each time this woman left the boss's office, her clothes appeared rumpled, and often her hair and makeup were a mess. This continued for months, so I eventually got used to it, simply ignored the matter, and conversed with both executives with imperturbable professionalism. For the full year that I worked at this firm, I never discussed the issue with anyone at the office or at home, even though I had a clear bird's-eye view of what was happening.

A few months prior to my departure from this firm, still young and naive in some respects, I was surprised when I overheard whisperings in the bathroom or at company functions about the two executives. It seemed that everyone in the firm knew full well what was going on. However, my integrity and professionalism was intact, as they had not heard it from me. Even if your peers engage in office tittle-tattle, you should not be the one to instigate it and, as much as possible, try not to get involved by voicing your opinion or spurring on the rumours. Your boss hired you and pays your salary, so despite his own shortcomings or amoral behaviour, as evidenced in this story, it is unprofessional of you to start rumours about him. If people who already know about his questionable behaviour seek confirmation from you, neither confirm nor deny it, and let it be known that you are unwilling to discuss any aspects of your boss's personal or private matters. This stance informs others that you do not condone that kind of behaviour, nor do you wish to be part of the rumour mill. Should your boss realize that he cannot trust you, it can be very difficult to regain his trust. In fact, it could be the beginning of the end.

One important caveat to note here is that the trust *must* be a two-way street. It can be very difficult for a secretary to consistently perform at a high standard if she works in an environment where she feels alienated by the very person she entrusts with her own professional development. I have always been up front at interviews by stating that the two things I look for in a potential employer are open communication and mutual respect. After conveying this to a potential employer who was an executive at a fairly small company, he used my prerequisite as a way to entice me into coming to work for him. He emphatically promised me that he would "always" keep me apprised of everything concerning our working relationship, organizational changes, and anything else of importance. No more than three months after I accepted his generous job offer, changes started to take place at the small firm, including the company's CEO being asked to step down by the board, and a number of senior executives being shown the door. Naturally, I was nervous about my decision to join a company that now seemed to be on very shaky ground. Just as he had asserted during my interview, my boss kept me up-to-date and informed me about what was transpiring at the firm, but only up to the point where the changes affected me directly. After the new management came on board they realigned various jobs, brought in their own team of staff, and made a large number of positions redundant, including mine. My boss did not forewarn me and was nowhere to be found. Instead, he took off on an extended vacation, leaving me to discover my fate directly from the new management. Although I recognized that his behaviour might have been motivated by shame, embarrassment, and helplessness, it gave me a great deal of insight and wisdom for the future. Clearly, I didn't do my due diligence in researching the firm. In hindsight, there was nothing more I could have done to ascertain whether the loyalty and trust in the relationship with my boss was truly reciprocal; I simply considered it a learning opportunity. Quite often bosses think it should be all about them, but this doesn't encourage loyalty and trust from their right hand – the secretary.

Communication Is Key

This may be an old-fashioned adage, but it is true. Communication is a key factor in a business environment. People cannot work in isolation in a business setting. The right hand must always be aware of what the left is doing. Working one-on-one with someone is impossible if you do not or cannot communicate. In fact, it is pointless, and the relationship is doomed to failure.

If you and your boss are finding it impossible to communicate or can't stand talking to each other, then a resolution needs to be found or the partnership needs to be dissolved, which means *you* must leave. A person I spoke to while doing research for this book informed me that the relationship with her previous employer, a female boss, reached a boiling point when they stopped talking to each other and would only converse via e-mail. When I asked about what had taken place, she told me that just as it can happen in a marriage, they had drifted apart and were both unwilling to make the extra effort to communicate. "Why?" I inquired. The secretary stated that her boss had consistently been disrespectful to her and that she had grown increasingly tired of it and now simply avoided speaking directly to her. *Aha!* I thought. This validated one of my two conditions for potential employees: mutual respect. It is impossible for the relationship between a secretary and her boss to work if there is lack of mutual respect. In this instance, the secretary felt that the boss treated her as if she were a "pea-brain." This, of course, was the secretary's account. I am almost certain that the female boss would have provided a different perspective on the situation. Inevitably, the secretary in question did quit the job.

When your work is exemplary, your boss will do everything possible to empower you. If you love your job, respect and like your boss, and are very happy with the organization you work for, but somehow you find that communication is lacking in your relationship with your boss, I recommend the following steps:

1. Set up a meeting and ask him to clarify his expectations of you and determine his preferred method of communicating with you.
2. Endeavour to include communication segments daily, or at least once or twice a week (depending on your boss's profile), by placing yourself on his calendar and using the time to update each other.
3. Suggest a regular breakfast or lunch meeting with him when his schedule is not hectic where you can catch up on all upcoming meetings, projects, organizational changes and announcements, priority meetings, and correspondence requiring action, set and meet deadlines, handle employee issues, and prepare for upcoming events. Making these meetings a regular occurrence will enhance your working relationship and avert surprises, crises, and misunderstandings.

You will find it easy to extend yourself in this manner only if you enjoy your job, respect your boss, and like the company you work for. Make every attempt to go the extra mile by anticipating your boss's needs and then exceed his expectations. If you work for an extremely busy senior executive, you could make every effort to alleviate his stress level by dealing with any mundane matters yourself, allowing him to concentrate on the important aspects of his job.

As a secretary, everyone relies on you to be familiar with all aspects of your boss's professional life – everything from his office neuroses or idiosyncrasies to how he takes his coffee or tea and even his favourite candy. At the beginning of the relationship, these are the little things you can make small talk with him about. Gradually, you will get to know everything you need to know about him professionally. If you are very good, you will be conversant with everything from his preferred airline and seating to his favourite baseball or hockey team.

As your relationship progresses and loyalty and trust are established on both sides, you will find that your boss will rely on you more and more, and you become a sort of confidante to him. When a relationship progresses to this stage, you become aware of the kind of power a secretary can possess, if she has the support of her manager. In this role, the power can be carte blanche, allowing you to make whatever changes you deem necessary in your boss's schedule and other matters. You may even find yourself attending some meetings on his behalf and reporting back to him. This rare portion of power is generally afforded to senior executive secretaries who support higher-ranking officers and directors of successful corporations.

Senior executives tend to be spread very thin in terms of commitments and travel and rely heavily on their personal secretaries to handle every aspect of their business with minimal supervision. Furthermore, they back up every decision their secretaries make, an empowering act that solidifies the position. To maintain this level of trust, you must keep the boss apprised of all the important matters you handle on his behalf. As time progresses, he will pass on more and more responsibility to you and come to value your judgement. When the relationship between you and your boss works, you will find your job extremely gratifying and fulfilling. You will quickly come to understand why so many secretaries love what they do and why the majority tend to stay loyal to one boss for many years, if not the rest of their career.

There are times, however, when you might find yourself working for an executive who is unaware of how to effectively utilize his secretarial resource. Such a boss might be reluctant to relinquish any of his own responsibilities to you because he has never had a secretary work for him, and as such he may be used to doing things for himself. Never look upon such behaviour as a reflection on you and your capabilities; the executive in question probably doesn't even realize what he is doing. To turn things around, you must take a proactive approach by persistently offering to take on some of the responsibilities from his "to-do" list and attentively handling them on his behalf. If you happen to be an experienced secretary, you could take the lead in educating and guiding him on how to make the most of your expertise, remembering that while he may not be conversant with the world of secretaries he is not a complete imbecile, and you'll soon win his respect.

Working for Multiple Bosses

If your role encompasses supporting the whole team in your department as well as the department head, you have your work cut out for you because you become not only the control centre for the department but also the focal point for all things administrative. In a large team environment you are likely to encounter a variety of issues, egos, and personality dynamics, and the only way to survive those conditions is to let neutrality guide your actions.

With most organizations slashing budgets, it is becoming more common for a secretary to have more than one boss to answer to. The relationship the secretary fosters with each of her bosses is unique because she not only must cater to each of her bosses' distinctive personalities and work requirements but also has to be sensitive to all their idiosyncrasies. She must treat each of her bosses fairly and provide superior service to each without bias. The secretary working in this type of environment needs to be adept at the game of office politics as it pertains to her particular role. This is not to say that she should be a pushover and allow each manager to make unrealistic demands upon her time. However, learning to manage each boss in a manner that is respectful and impartial can be challenging for an inexperienced secretary.

To be successful in a multiple-boss scenario, you must be an excellent communicator. More often than not, one boss forgets that you support others who require the same level of service that he demands of you and becomes possessive about his work and your time. Quite often he doesn't even want to be reminded that his is sharing you with one or two others; he just wants his work done when he wants it done. A secretary who is intimidated by such behaviour will have a difficult time being successful in this role unless she learns to manage expectations on her time and work output. If you find yourself in this situation, you will need to skilfully and regularly remind your superiors that there is only one of you supporting many of them.

As long as you are firm and respectful, your bosses will slowly come to realize that they cannot have whatever they want at any given moment but must learn to share their secretarial resource. The more they are reminded of this in a respectful manner, the better the situation for the secretary, and eventually they will be well trained.

A seasoned secretary will suggest regular team meetings where her workload and support to the team is discussed and any serious issues are tabled and resolved professionally. To be successful in such a role, if you support multiple bosses, you would be well advised to keep your feelings to yourself about which boss is your favourite, because if he resigns or is fired you could find yourself in a very precarious position. Clarifying priorities between the bosses will also go a long way in making your work life easier.

Male or Female Bosses

Having a boss and secretary of the same gender can be a good or bad arrangement. The personalities involved determine the success of these relationships. Having a boss of the same gender can lead to volatile and complicated relationships if the two individuals are too much alike. Given the ideally supportive nature of the secretarial role, if the parties engage in a personal power struggle, the relationship is doomed to failure.

I don't believe that we can generalize about the gender issue anymore, unless the job is in a country where women don't have rights that are equal to their male counterparts. I have known many male bosses with old-fashioned views about secretaries that they refuse to change or compromise. These bosses will only hire secretaries willing to work under their defined rules of engagement. Similarly, I have worked for oppressive female bosses who take their power too seriously and treat their secretaries just as shabbily (if not worse) as their male counterparts. Ultimately it is all about personalities and in my view has less to do with gender than it has to do with the individual's will to dominate, and his or her fear and insecurity.

With some secretarial experience behind you, the decision to work for a male or female boss will depend on past experiences and first impressions. If you have had some unpleasant experiences supporting female bosses, you may decide to never work for another, but few secretaries can afford to make this distinction. Try to give each situation a fair chance. Where women are concerned, I think it is evident during the interviewing process if the two personalities can form a true partnership. If you are a junior secretary just starting out in your career, I am sure that you won't mind working for a male or female boss because you really will not have a particular frame of reference.

Generally, if you are female and a female boss chooses to hire you, you have little to worry about. If something about you doesn't appeal to the female boss or she is unsure about you, she is not likely to hire you unless the pool of candidates is paltry, and then she might take a chance on you. An employment agency once sent me to a job interview with a prestigious firm for a position supporting a senior vice president. I found out at the interview that the senior VP was female and the interviewer let her name slip. It turned out I knew who this potential boss was, as she had been one of the VPs in a company that I had left two years before. The next day I called the agency and asked them to withdraw my name from the candidate pool for that particular position. While I had nothing against this female VP personally, I had an uneasy feeling about working one-on-one with her – in my view, our personalities were not compatible. The feeling turned out to be mutual, because the VP informed the agency that she was very interested in hiring me but that she wanted to give it a trial run by having me come in on a "temp to permanent" basis. This was a fair determination on her part. We both recognized the potentially prickly situation of having two very strong-willed women whose personalities just did not mesh trying to work together. Needless to say, I declined the proposition and the decision came easily for me. At the same time, however, it is unlikely that at the beginning of my career this situation would have mattered.

On the flip side of this coin, a friend of mine worked for a female boss who was so supportive and wonderful that I couldn't help but be envious. The two were extremely close, and their mutual respect was evident. They would regularly be seen going out for lunch together, and today that secretary now works alongside her former boss as a customer service manager for the same firm. However, some of the secretaries I interviewed for this book stated that they believed female bosses are generally not very supportive of their career goals. One secretary even said that a female boss had advised her to hide her ambitions and pursue them in secret. I consider any kind of generalization about gender unfair because I am also aware of a number of secretaries who prefer female bosses over male bosses. There really is no secret formula; the relationship is dependent on personalities, trust, and respect, regardless of gender. When I look back at my own career, I have had the best and the worst of both male and female bosses. Each work experience had its merits, helped me grow, and prepared me for the next situation. To this day I hold dear the memory of two wonderful female university professors who I worked for simultaneously many years ago, and I would gladly repeat the experience.

A word of caution regarding your relationship with your boss: neither of you should entertain crossing the line into the realm of close friendship or a more intimate connection. If your boss's behaviour changes and goes beyond what you consider professional, put a stop to it immediately. Never encourage or tolerate anything you deem inappropriate, even if it costs you your job. In my own experience, it is very easy to become good friends with your boss, especially if you are the same gender. However, bosses *cannot* have it both ways, expecting you to be a friend when it suits them and then proceeding to pull rank when they want something done. This is not friendship, and a smart secretary avoids this type of scenario altogether.

The Ideal Work Environment

Remember that being a secretary is incredibly fulfilling and fun as long as it is a good fit for the employer and, more importantly, for you. With experience comes confidence, and with confidence comes proficiency, which leads to job satisfaction. But job satisfaction is not always easy to come by in the secretarial world, because it hinges on many factors, including the organizational culture, the business model, the politics, the boss (how he treats you, his expectations of you, and his level of respect for you as an individual), the job description, and that all-important compensation. Your journey is only as successful as your superiors and your own ambition allow it to be. Sometimes your tenacity and drive for success can be unwelcome and viewed as impertinent career aggression.

Looking back at all the places, companies, and people I have worked for, I have come to believe that the ideal working environment is one where the climate is supportive and friendly, where people have both respect and humility, and where they trust one another. Examples of such an environment would consist of at least some or all of the following characteristics:

The Ideal Office

- It is a threat-free environment – people are not afraid to speak up for fear of ramifications.
- People are not afraid to make mistakes; they learn from them without reprisals.
- There is mutual respect among colleagues.
- Everyone comes to work every day with renewed vigour and a desire to excel.
- Camaraderie and morale is high, and teamwork is apparent.
- Turnover and sick absences are low.
- Communication is viewed as a key element for success by all.
- Creativeness and thinking outside of the box is welcome and applauded.

The boss …

- is a natural leader who leads by example.
- genuinely walks the walk.
- possesses enviable personal integrity.

- has an open-door policy.
- is guided by honesty and fairness in all his dealings.
- gives useful feedback without malice.
- is held in very high esteem and respected by all.
- is not blinded in his dealings by personal ambition or an agenda.
- welcomes constructive criticism.
- recognizes good work.
- doesn't rule with an iron fist or by intimidation.

Organizational Guiding Principles

- There is zero tolerance for employees or managers who have engaged in harassment, discrimination, or misuse of their position of authority.
- There are equal opportunities of advancement for everyone.
- Malicious gossip and any activity that is not conducive to a good work environment is prohibited.
- Organizational values and claims of equality and fairness are carried through.
- The organization recognizes that its "people" (translation: employees) are the most valuable asset it has.

Bully Bosses

What can you do if your boss is a bully? What kind of behaviour by a boss constitutes bullying, anyway? Well, if your boss possesses the not-so-pleasant traits listed below, then you need to decide whether you want to confront him about his behaviour, report his treatment of you to the human resources department, or quit. The third option is the most common route that most secretaries take if the environment they work in turns sour, but this doesn't always help your successor, as the boss will never learn. However, as a secretary it is very difficult to garner any support for accusations against your boss, unless there already are other numerous complaints about him, in which case your grievance might not fall on deaf ears. I have even known some secretaries to just let it roll off their backs and continue as if nothing ever happened. The course of action you choose to take against a bully remains at your discretion, depending on your personal situation. However, it deserves mention in this publication because bullying does happen in offices and can reach a boiling point. In 2004, a secretary in the United Kingdom sued and won damages of £800,000 (about $1.24 million USD) after allegedly enduring relentless bullying within a department at Deutsche Bank. Describing what she went through, she stated that it "nearly drove her to the point of a mental breakdown."[27] An environment where oppressive behaviour is common is often described as a "constraining" or "unhealthy" working environment.

Characteristics of a Bully Boss

1. If your boss doesn't treat you with respect and talks to you as if you are dense, then that is disrespectful behaviour. He is categorizing you as a less significant person by his standards.
2. If he continuously loses his temper for the slightest mishap and then takes it out on you, he is an office bully.
3. If he raises his voice in front of your peers and belittles you about something he doesn't feel was done properly, he is definitely a self-engrossed tyrant.
4. If he terrorizes everyone in the office because he doesn't get his way, that is far from being conducive to a healthy working environment, and the effects of this behaviour can be long lasting and damage your self-esteem.
5. If you fear your boss to such an extent that you find yourself trembling in his presence, you can assume that you're dealing with a bully.
6. If you are subjected to verbal abuse with statements such as, "You are stupid" or "You are useless," you need to document the incident and immediately consult an impartial employee support group within the organization or the company ombudsman for advice. If neither exists, you have no choice but to report the matter to the head of human resources, and if you have witnesses to the incident who are willing to back

27 Adam Fresco, "£800,000 payout for bullied City secretary," *The Times*, accessed August 3, 2006, http://www.thetimes.co.uk/tto/law/article2215353.ece.

> you up, that is even better. If you work in a small firm, your options might be limited. Another secretary I interviewed for this book shared how her female boss was so persistently rude and verbally abusive to her that she just stopped going to work, thus quitting. When I asked her to elaborate, she stated that she worked for a private, one-person business. The head of this enterprise, a female entrepreneur, was well known for her temper. This particular secretary believed that nobody could be that bad and took the job. The verbal torment and belittling that she endured was unbelievable, she told me. The boss would frequently call her "stupid" and would ask her snide, rhetorical questions like, "Do you think before you do anything?" or "Do you have a brain in that thick head of yours?" The secretary stated that on one particular day she received this verbal abuse persistently over the telephone when the boss's off-site meeting hadn't gone well. She never returned to the premises, nor did she convey that she was quitting; she just stopped going to work in protest.

Mutual respect is crucial between an executive and his secretary. If your boss shows you no respect, either confront him with your feelings or find another job where you will get the respect that you deserve. In addition, if you find that you simply cannot bring yourself to look at your boss with any semblance of respect due to his attitude towards you, secretaries in general or some other reason that conflicts with your personal value system, ask yourself two crucial questions:

1. Do I like my job, my boss, and the company?
2. Am I happy to be here and fulfilled in my current role?

If the answer is a resounding no, you need to reconsider your position and your future.

There is no excuse for arrogance, verbal abuse, bullying, or bad manners. You should never retaliate or behave in the same manner or the situation will simply erupt, and like it or not, *you* will be the one to lose out or get fired. Maintain your integrity and professionalism while looking for an exit, and leave with your dignity intact.

Characteristics of an Unhealthy Work Environment

- A mistake is treated like a cardinal sin.
- People abruptly stop talking when the boss arrives.
- People always work with one eye on the clock.
- Everyone disappears from the office as soon as the clock strikes quitting time.
- People are afraid to speak up or voice good ideas for fear of ridicule.
- Everyone is at ease and happy when the boss is away.
- Unprofessional conduct such as bullying, favouritism, and blatant gossip mongering is tolerated without reprisals.

Sometimes bosses can affect your professional career in other ways besides bullying. Many years ago, I approached a female boss expressing a desire to transfer to the company's human resources department, and she promised to keep an eye out for the right opportunity. Later, an executive vice president in the same company approached me with a promotion that meant I would be working for him instead. As I prepared to move into my new role, I accidentally came across a performance evaluation authored by my current boss. She was expressing her dissatisfaction about losing me, which was flattering, but what infuriated me was the fact that she blatantly stated that I was such a proficient EA (executive assistant) she had been hesitant to help me progress into the HR field because she would have had to deal with some other, inefficient secretary. It's needless to say that I was horrified by this discovery and lost all respect for her as a person. This boss was, according to her own admission, praising me on the one hand while blocking my career advancement out of pure self-interest on the other. Many bosses are guilty of being unenthusiastic to promote or assist their secretaries in career advancement because it disturbs the equilibrium of the team and their well-established operational structure. As a secretary, you need to be in the driver's seat of your career at all times, and it is quite all right to quietly question (in the back of your mind) your boss's motives when you ask for his or her help in career advancement.

Let's take a look at another scenario. One secretary whom I knew quite well in London, England, often told me of the horrors of her position at the time and surprised me further by insisting on staying put. She was extremely well paid, but her top-rate salary came at a price. Her boss apparently had a vicious personality and was often heard spewing out verbal abuse to anyone who made a mistake. For the purpose of this book, I will call this secretary Susan. Everyone in her department had both witnessed and been at the receiving end of the wrath of the man in charge. It became the norm in the course of a business day. Prior to Susan coming on board, her boss had gone through sixteen secretaries in one year! Some quit of their own accord, and others he fired, usually after one or two days of their working for him. So what was special about Susan?

Susan wasn't staying because she was enticed by the money, but she differed from her predecessors in that she truly believed that there was some good in the man she worked for. She viewed his ranting and raving as a facade for his own insecurities and was not afraid of him. Her boss did tell her she was fired on many occasions, but Susan always returned to work the following day as if nothing had happened, with the unapologetic goal of proving him wrong through her efficiency and pleasant demeanour, in spite of the torrent of verbal abuse. Indeed, what Susan did took nerves of steel and a deep sense of self. While I have stated that there is absolutely no need for a secretary to endure any kind of abuse, as long as you can handle the situation you can continue undeterred, and only you will know if and when it is time to leave.

Another boss in an organization where I once worked ruled the office as his own personal fiefdom, and his management style was one of intimidation. He would snap at the slightest cause of irritation and was always on the lookout for anyone in the small firm to slip up, and then he would immediately point this out. I could see that he was a "fault-finder" personality type who relished doing so! What was humorous to me was the fact that below his outgoing e-mail signature line was the company's supposed set of values – "Integrity, Trust, and Respect." Clearly, his personal conduct did not match the company's set of values and principles.

So what can a secretary do when her work environment is made toxic by a bully boss? Social change only takes place if the groups involved do not simply lie down and accept the status quo. Refusing to work in an offensive office environment, where the use of racial and religious slurs, threats, verbal abuse, and other demeaning remarks or discriminatory conduct is tolerated is one way to start effecting change. I was intrigued to learn that one company I had previously worked at and left precisely for that reason was maligned by a long line of administrative staff (their preferred label) who left the company consecutively in the space of a few months. Each week I kept hearing that one or two secretaries had quit, and this happened so many times that I was embarrassed for the firm. By doing a couple of exit interviews, some members of the organization learned that the environment had to change or the turnover would continue. The company did not treat people well, especially the secretaries, and I can only hope that they came to realize this in the end.

The majority of secretaries are well trained and extensively skilled at what they do, and yet their existence is often taken for granted and the significance of their role disregarded. Certain contingents of managers who understand very little about a secretary's role have a habitual tendency to be condescending when liaising with secretaries, that is, if they even bother to acknowledge their presence. A boss who is unsure of himself or how to maximize the role of his secretary will micromanage her to cover his own incompetence, or he will simply alienate her, defeating the purpose of hiring her in the first place. Given the level of intelligence required to ensure strict adherence to corporate guidelines in all aspects of a secretary's role, managers who treat secretaries as second- or third-class citizens only highlight their ignorance with such behaviour. A smart secretary recognizes this and simply shrugs it off as chauvinistic and conceited ignorance. It never ceased to amaze me, the number of so-called senior managers who would literally look past me or ignore me on account of my job title alone. Their behaviour reinforced what I viewed as their uninformed assumption that I was an inconsequential person who did not deserve their respect or as simple a gesture as saying "hello."

Going into this profession, you need to be aware of all the intricacies of this kind of work. The best advice I can proffer on how to deal with each unpleasant situation is to ensure that you pass these five self-tests prior to any form of reaction or response to a conflict situation:

1. Am I conducting myself with professionalism?
2. Am I behaving with integrity?
3. Am I being kind and understanding?
4. Am I being ethical?
5. Am I compromising my values and standards of work?

Dealing with Prejudice and/or Discrimination

In my long career as a secretary, I always approached every situation with a positive attitude, believing the glass is always half full. I never encountered much discrimination, and in cases where I thought it was a possibility, I never allowed myself to find out. What do I mean by this? As I stressed in earlier chapters of this book, you should always interview a prospective employer with as much vigour and caution as they do you. You should also align yourself with people, especially employers, who share your values and treat you with respect. If you have foreboding feelings about a company, situation or employer, you may need to reevaluate. As a member of a visible minority group, I had a multitude of barriers to break through before I could declare myself to be a success story. I was brought up to believe that I mattered and was no different from anyone else, and that has always been my attitude in any working environment. But even that stalwart attitude was shaken when I overhead my work colleagues discussing me using racial slurs or discriminatory language, which I found extremely hurtful. Depending on your own set of goals, values, and personality, you can accept the situation or you can fight to correct it. Where secretaries are concerned, it all depends on your outlook on life and your understanding of your role in the organization. Sometimes it is better to walk away because there is always a much better situation devoid of prejudice or discrimination if you are open to exploring the possibility.

The view held by a certain contingent of ignorant managers is prejudicial. For them, all secretaries must be female, and they are brainless beings whose role in life is to answer the telephone, make coffee, and type dictated letters. This prejudicial view is conveyed by the manner in which the perpetrator (boss) treats his secretary, in a lack of career or monetary recognition, in stereotyping, and in open disrespect based on age, gender, race, disability, religion, and assumed level of education. In the course of writing this book, some people have admitted to me that they assume secretaries have no real education, and that all a secretary knows how to do is take orders and type. Well, if that is not prejudice or stereotyping, then I don't know what is. However, this argument is as old as time, and the only way forward is for secretaries to counter this prejudicial behaviour by standing up for themselves and speaking out against discrimination, bigotry, and prejudice. While writing this book, I continued to hear secretaries referred to pejoratively as "admins" or "admin person/people," as if we were from another planet. As a tenured secretary listening to someone use this term, this sounded very offensive to me because the correct term is "administrative assistant" or "admin assistant."

On the flip side, a male secretary working in Europe gave me some insight into his experience working in this profession years ago. The young man, who I will call Steve, informed me that he faced immense discrimination while looking for work. He was especially bitter about the fact that he lost what he called plum secretarial jobs to female secretaries with less experience. When I asked how he knew that those female secretaries had less experience, he stated that he knew some of them personally, and that others were previous colleagues. Steve was even more irritated with employment agencies because he felt that they weren't honest with him; they would promise to find him jobs, but he usually never heard from them again.

When I asked why he chose this profession, he replied that after completing secondary school he spent some time doing compulsory military service, and it was during this period that he also discovered administrative work. When he completed his service, he enrolled in a two-year secretarial training program. The fact that Steve was the lone male in a class with twenty-five females was the icing on the cake, as far as he was concerned. Unfortunately, when he graduated from his secretarial study program, all his classmates found work almost immediately, except for him. No one would hire him, and the reason for this, according to Steve, was because he was a man. As much as Steve wanted to be a secretary, the fact that no one would hire him demoralized him, so he gave up on his secretarial dream. Steve spoke of this happening during the mid-1990s, and it is entirely possible that his experience would be starkly different and much more positive today. It is interesting, however, that an online survey on gender pay differentials conducted by the management consultancy firm OD&M discovered that "for secretarial staff, the gender wage differential was to women's advantage,"[28] which indicates to me that change in this area is still slower than it should be.

Countering Sexual Harassment

Sexual harassment is illegal in most countries and is not a matter to be taken lightly. It is an insidious form of control characterized by unwanted attention based on sex, gender, or sexual orientation. The perpetrators are not confined to one gender, social, or corporate status, and the mode used can be verbal, written, physical, graphic, or a combination of all four. Once it begins, sexual harassment will not go away if ignored; it will only escalate. It needs to be rooted out from all organizations, irrespective of who is involved and their stature within the organization. Depending on company policy and how seriously they take the case,

28 Domencio Paparella, "Gender pay differentials examined," *Eurofound*, accessed March 4, 2007, http://www.eurofound.europa.eu/eiro/2001/04/inbrief/it0104181n.html.

the outcome of a sexual harassment investigation can damage one or both careers involved.

In another headline-making case from the United Kingdom in 2009, a woman was awarded £9,000 in damages for what was described in *The Telegraph* newspaper as "systematic and continuous" sexual harassment.[29] The lone female employee and office administrator of a plumbing company alleged that she was treated abhorrently; she claimed that she was ordered to clean an overflowing male lavatory and the kitchens on a daily basis, and that the abuse extended to name-calling, which stripped her of her self-confidence.

Conversely, back in 1996 a male typist in England lost his case against an employment agency he accused of sexual discrimination.[30] Contending bias on the basis of his gender, he lost the case because the tribunal found inconsistencies in his account of what transpired. The interesting aspect of the story was the fact that male secretaries are just as sensitive to discrimination and harassment as women. Employers and employment agencies need to consider this when dealing with either gender.

Should you fall prey to sexual harassment of any kind, I recommend you take the following actions:

1. After the first incident, firmly inform the assailant to stop and tell him that you do not appreciate his behaviour.
2. Document the event(s), giving as detailed an account of the incident as is possible. Note the dates, locations, and times of each incident and the names of people who witnessed it.
3. If the behaviour persists, write a letter to the assailant and keep a copy for your own files. Inform the other person how

29 "Secretary called 'bitch' and made to scrub male toilets wins damages," *Telegraph,* accessed January 19, 2010, http://www.telegraph.co.uk/news/uknews/4689236/Secretary-called-bitch-and-made-to-scrub-male-toilets-wins-damages.html.

30 "Super-skilled male secretary loses agency sex bias claim," *The Independent,* accessed January 22, 2010, http://www.independent.co.uk/news/superskilled-male-secretary-loses-agency-sex-bias-claim-1324686.html.

his behaviour makes you feel and threaten to take action if it ever happens again.

4. If the assailant continues to harass you, clearly there is a problem. Gather any documentation that you have to support your claim and take the matter to the appropriate person in the human resources department, or the head of the company if it is a small firm. If you work for the big boss himself, go to the head of the human resources department and show that person everything. The HR executive is likely to knock some sense into the assailant, as he or she understands these matters and knows how they can cause bad publicity for the company.
5. If the assailant dares to persist or takes action to get you fired, write another letter to him and copy the human resources department stating that you will be taking appropriate legal action as, despite your best efforts, the matter is not being resolved.
6. Immediately contact a lawyer and let him or her guide you through the process. If you decide to sue the company, you will probably be dismissed, as it will no longer be possible for you to work for the company at the same time.

Summary

- Do not overstep the familiarity boundary with your boss.
- Be extremely loyal to your boss without compromise, even if he doesn't always deserve it.
- Remember that your primary role is to make your boss's work life easier.
- Be trustworthy and let trust be synonymous with you.
- Look upon the boss's wife as a friend rather than a foe.
- Communication is key, and it is a two-way street.
- To be respected, one must be respectful.
- Learn to be assertive rather than aggressive.
- Maintain your integrity.
- Extend the same courtesy and respect to multiple bosses as you would to one boss, without partiality.

- Sit in the driver's seat of your career and do not always rely on your boss to facilitate your career advancement.
- Document and report any incidents of sexual harassment, discrimination or prejudice.
- Give 100 percent and do the best work you can.
- Remember, you can easily be replaced.
- If the boss or the company is disrespecting or mistreating you, it's definitely time to move on.

Chapter 10: The Final Word

So you want to be a secretary? What sort of secretary would you like to be? Have you gone through the decision-making process to plan out your career? Are you already working as a secretary? If so, would you classify yourself as an average or elite secretary? Does your professional conduct align with some of the values, competencies, guidelines, and recommended rules of engagement outlined in this book?

The most common question in any interview is, "Where do you see yourself in five years' time?" I always struggled with that question at the beginning of my career because frankly, I did not know the answer. What I did know was that I wanted to be a top-notch secretary and acquire as much diverse experience as possible. Twenty years later I can boldly and triumphantly state that I accomplished that goal. So I ask you the same question. Where do you want this career to lead you? Allow me to remind you about the amazing journey you are about to embark on.

Every experience you encounter on your secretarial journey, good or bad, makes you a better secretary. There are so many secretaries I am acquainted with who are tenured and working for very high-net-worth companies and the most wonderful of bosses. One such acquaintance is so highly regarded by her boss that he cannot make a decision without consulting her. Every single morning he buys two cups of coffee on his way up to his office – one for him and one for his secretary. He showers her with gifts, and she spends a great deal of her spare time at some of the most luxurious spas, or using the large number of gift cards her boss gives to her. Another acquaintance works for a senior executive at a highly successful oil and gas company in Canada. She has spent her entire career as a secretary working for this one executive.

As he moved up the chain of command and switched companies, his stipulation was always that they both must join any firm as a twosome. The matter of deciding who his executive secretary will be has always been non-negotiable. There is only one person he trusts and she "must" be part of his offer package. They fly around the world in the company jet attending various company meetings, conferences, and events. Her own compensation package beats that of most regular managers in an average-sized firm. Her postsecondary education has been sponsored by her employer, and although she could hang up her secretarial hat and pursue another career on account of the bachelor's degree she has acquired, she chooses not to and has told me firmly that she is staying put. This honour is not reserved for her alone. The other executive secretaries at the firm working at the same level enjoy the same privileges with their executive bosses. It is not surprising that none of them are willing to quit their positions, and I am almost certain they will hang on until they retire.

Working in London, England, in the 1990s, one boss treated me so especially well that I have never forgotten it, mainly because no other boss has come even close to the generosity and kindness of that employer. Not only did I often find unique gifts and thank you cards at my desk, but I also received flowers as a matter of course and for any excuse that this boss could find. Birthdays, Christmas, a welcome back to the office after illness, for a job well done and, yes, even on Valentine's Day. I would order and send flowers to his wife, but I would also get a small bouquet from my boss, and the note always read, "Have a wonderful Valentine's Day. You are a star!" I can recall one incident when I headed into the elevator on the main floor, and as the elevator doors closed, I just managed to catch sight of my boss walking towards the main entrance with a large bouquet of flowers in tow. Later, as he placed the vase on my desk, I was mildly amused but very appreciative. Other secretaries at the firm felt that the flowers and gifts were a bit over the top, but I never saw any reason to complain. Every day I bounced into that office, joyful and happy to be where I was. I absolutely loved my job. As stated in a previous chapter, being a personal assistant (PA) in London, England, particularly (and many other places, I am sure) is highly regarded and admired and comes with many wonderful perks, not least of which are high pay and genuine appreciation from bosses who understand the value of a good assistant. If you can recall the story that I cited in chapter 9 about a personal assistant in London who was awarded £800,000 in damages for the horrific bullying that she allegedly endured, it is worth noting that her settlement was extremely high. My own thoughts about the large settlement were echoed by a writer for *The Times* of London, who wrote, "Her settlement would lead us to believe that her total annual compensation package must have been somewhere close to the £100,000 per year mark!"[31] A large sum indeed, and when you convert these figures to Canadian or American currency, it should be evident why I have consistently stated that being a PA in the United Kingdom, particularly a top-earning one, is nothing to frown upon. There are managers who earn half that amount in North America, let alone the United Kingdom or parts of Europe.

So the question isn't, "Do you want to be a secretary and why?" The question is, "Why not?" In addition to all your training in this field and other education you may have attained, if you have read this entire book, you are now well and truly ready to pursue this profession and be a huge success at it. The majority of secretaries I am acquainted with are incredibly privileged in their roles and have a tremendous sense of job fulfilment. Besides travelling regularly with their bosses, planning events in the most exotic locations around the country, and, for a lucky few, around the world, typically falls within a secretary's purview.

Another secretary interviewed for this book advised that she feels incredibly lucky and privileged. This secretary works solely from home, which allows her to be a stay-at-home working mom. She earns a very good salary, has great benefits, and is very content to continue in this manner for as long as is possible.

---

31 Adam Fresco, "Secretary bullied in 'department from Hell' is awarded £800,000," *The Times*, retrieved August 3, 2006, http://www.thetimes.co.ok/tto/career/article1793832.ece.

As I conducted my research for this book, I also came to realize that many people are completely unaware of the perks that come with most secretarial roles, especially for senior executive secretaries considered to be at the top of their game. Did you know that some secretaries have company-paid parking (I certainly did for a large portion of my secretarial working life in Canada), while others have wardrobe allowances, drive company vehicles, or hold executive memberships at exclusive gyms and carry the latest in personal communication devices, all at the company's expense? The list is long and eyebrow-raising to the uninformed. On top of all that, being a secretary is a marvellously fulfilling career when one is matched to the right boss and the right company.

Now that you know what to expect and have gained some insight into what I outlined in the preface as "a day in the life of a secretary," I hope that as you embark on this professional journey you are well prepared. I also stated in the preface that the reason I wrote this book was not to name names or dish the dirt but to delve deeper and describe the real experiences that a new secretary is likely to encounter on the job and to provide practical tools for handling the ambiguous aspects of the job for working secretaries. The experiences that were highlighted in this book were presented as examples to show the repercussions of such actions, but you will notice that no real names were cited. I cannot stress this enough: discretion is imperative in the secretarial profession.

For those of you who are already working as a secretary in some capacity, I hope that you are not only well armed for dealing with the nuances of the job but also reminded of all the wonderful reasons you chose to work as a secretary. For the secretaries currently in training for this splendid career, fear not. There are upsides and downsides to every job, and I have highlighted some of the best and worst situations you are likely to encounter. It is very unlikely that you will experience the negative aspects too often and highly likely that you will enjoy the positives frequently. The worst thing anyone can do is join this profession with a sense of hesitancy, mediocrity, and reservation. You must love the idea of being a secretary if you are to attain the pinnacle – "elite" status. It is amazing how our perception of who we are is exactly how the world perceives us; *we* teach the world how to view and treat us. If you have the education and training, the understanding of what is expected of you and the tenacity to be the best, then success as a secretary is virtually guaranteed for you. All that I am attempting to do here is to reinforce for you, the reader, the importance of carefully planning your career, setting the highest professional standards for yourself and making sure you have the capability to steer your career in exactly the direction that you want it to go. You cannot rely on others to do that for you. You need to be clear about the direction you are headed in and the type of industry that will hold your interest and bring you the most satisfaction.

Although the label has changed from secretary to administrative assistant or variations of the word "assistant," the core function of a secretary has not changed; rather, it has been enhanced. In an article titled "Administrative Personnel Taking on More Responsibilities," reporter Derek Sankey, writing for the *Calgary Herald* newspaper, observed, "Gone are the days of just getting coffee and answering the phones. In small companies, administrative professionals are often the backbone of the entire business, wearing many hats throughout a typical day."[32] Secretaries who understand their role fare a lot better than those who learn as they go. Know going in what to expect from the job, the company, and the profession overall, and the ride will be that much easier and more enjoyable. The secretary will always be relevant, but her role and title may continue to change and evolve.

While male secretaries continue to be in the minority, I predict that the playing field will begin to level off by the end of this century. Male nurses and male models were once a novelty but are not anymore, and I envision the same for male secretaries.

During a recession or an economic downturn, secretaries are the last people who need to worry about job security because they are the lifeblood of an organization, and unless their boss is made redundant

32 Derek Sankey, "Administrative personnel taking on more responsibilities," *The Calgary Herald*, July 7, 2010, accessed July 26, 2010, http://www.working.com.

or the company itself falls on extremely hard times and collapses, the secretarial position, although not immune, is rarely impacted.

There are times, however, when the corporate world with all its politics and disparate cultures can be repressive, isolating, and all-consuming, making it feel as though the company represents the entire world. When this happens, you can lose sight of the fact that there is another world outside of the corporation you are working for. If it is time to make a change, do so with your dignity and integrity intact, even if you leave under less than ideal circumstances. Learn from the experience and simply move on with minimal fuss or fanfare. If you find yourself working in a toxic environment, the power struggles you are caught up in, along with the competitiveness, jealousy, bullying tactics, gossiping, and never-ending innuendos can all seem overwhelming for an inexperienced secretary, but they need not be. I can personally attest to the fact that more often than not, the grass is indeed greener on the other side, if you have the courage to step out in order to discover it.

When a secretary lands the ideal job with a supportive boss in an organization that nurtures its employees and strives to offer a great place to work, all that the lucky secretary needs to do is buckle up and enjoy the ride. The perks that come with working for a great boss in a great company are incredible and are a source of envy for non-secretaries. It is no accident that many secretaries I know have worked for the same company and remained loyal to one boss for most of their careers. Leaving a great situation is difficult; I should know. I once left a wonderful boss, position, and company for what I considered a large pay hike at another firm. No more than three weeks into the new position I realized that I had made a horrendous mistake and that the money itself mattered little. I was unhappy and learning each and every day that this was not the right place for me. Within six months I was back with my previous employer, earning the same as I had been before I left, but this time truly happy to be where I was. For a while I regretted my initial decision to leave an agreeable situation for the almighty dollar, but upon reflection I realized that I had needed to learn the lesson that money isn't everything, and that there are many other crucial factors to consider before making drastic career moves. Secretaries who have learned this lesson earlier in their careers know a good thing when they find it and cannot be blamed for staying put. Caution, however, need not translate into fear, despondency, and lack of ambition. My message here is simple: weigh the pros and cons very carefully before making the decision to leave a favourable situation, but don't hang around in a toxic situation, either. Ambition is good, as long as it is "smart ambition."

As a secretary, you must counter the uninformed notion that we are a vacuous group who exist in an organization merely to sustain the administrative function that is necessary for every business to run smoothly. The assumption is that we are clueless where it comes to real business – a notion based on ignorance and arrogance that is basically untrue. Working as a senior executive assistant in Canada, I managed to run my own image consultancy business successfully for a decade in tandem with my full-time secretarial career. To be truly "elite," take advantage of every opportunity to learn about your company from the operations side of the business so you can understand how its bottom line is affected by various market forces. When your company provides tuition reimbursement, take advantage of that opportunity to advance your education. Never stop learning. No amount of learning is ever wasted; it will stand you in very good stead one day in the future.

If you ever find yourself working as a temporary secretary, take advantage of the opportunity to learn about the job, the boss, the company, and the culture. More importantly, enjoy making lasting friendships, business connections, and the freedom that comes with being a free agent. When invited to convert your temporary contract to permanent employment, be sure to evaluate the merits and shortcomings of the situation. A temporary employee is always in the driver's seat.

There is so much more to the secretarial role, but the focus of this book was, as promised, to deal with the behind-the-scenes work life of a secretary, to focus on what makes secretaries great, to offer solid advice on how to handle difficult situations, to put a spotlight on the role itself, and to examine thoroughly the nuances of the corporate world and how they impact both the beginner and senior secretary. A full chapter was dedicated to office politics (chapter 5) because they are integral to the role. All secretaries must be savvy about the office politics within their particular organization. They are a fact of office life in every organization, big or small. Understand that you cannot change or do anything about office politics, so just accept them and play along in order to survive, remembering that taking flight may not necessarily solve your problem. You could wind up running for the rest of your career, only to find office politics of a different kind waiting for you at each new job.

Secretaries who join any organization will have to learn to play by the "existing" rules, whether they are a novice or experienced. Just like professional sport, you must understand the rules before you begin to play. You must practice. You must persevere. You must correct your mistakes and learn from them. You must play to win!

Summary

- Go through the decision-making process. Take the time to evaluate why you want to be a secretary and in what industry.
- Master the art of résumé writing or engage a professional; you cannot afford to make a bad first impression.
- Follow the guidelines for submission as set out by the employer. If the employer stipulates that all applications should be submitted via an online application tool, you must oblige.
- Format your cover letter exactly as the résumé. Use the same paper, font, and font size.
- Bad grammar and spelling will negatively affect your application.
- Never attend an interview unprepared.
- At an interview, remember to evaluate the employer according to your own suitability checklist.
- Request and study the job description prior to accepting a position.
- When you join a company, the onus is on you to try and fit into the existing culture.

- Be wary of unsavoury office personalities and be prepared to respond appropriately to the challenges posed by these individuals.
- Always be aware of the VIPs in your organization; they expect you to know who they are.
- Study the hierarchy of your organization. It will make your job easier.
- The telephone is the most crucial apparatus in any organization, so polish your telephone etiquette.
- Be respectful of your employer's property and proprietary information.
- Time management and organizational skills are the foundation of a secretary's role and ultimate success.
- Do not let perfectionism guide your success barometer. You must be adaptable and willing to adjust or compromise your success record for the good of all. By all means, you must set goals and work hard to accomplish them, but be realistic – nobody is perfect.
- Working as a temporary employee has its advantages and disadvantages, but it is a great choice for those who want exposure to many different industries.
- A good fit, communication, and an element of trust are some of the building blocks for a successful working relationship between a boss and his secretary.
- A secretary should never tolerate bullying behaviour of any kind in the workplace.
- In order to survive, a secretary must understand and learn how to play the office politics in her particular organization.
- Continuous development and education is the key to success, so learn, grow, and never stop challenging yourself.
- A world without secretaries is improbable, and the bosses whose professional lives depend on their secretaries will be the first to attest to this fact, so enjoy!

Glossary

AA – administrative assistant

BBC – British Broadcasting Corporation

Blog – a Web log or journal maintained and published on the Internet

CEO – chief executive officer

CFO – chief financial officer

COO – chief operating officer

Clocking – keenly observing the time that someone comes in and leaves the office

Clubbing – the regular patronage of night clubs

CPS – Certified Professional Secretaries Examination

CV – curriculum vitae

Dictaphone – dictation machine

EA – executive assistant

Encl. – enclosures

GBP – Great British pound

Google – an Internet search engine

HR – human resources

HRA – human resources advisor

IAAP – International Association of Administrative Professionals

IT – information technology

Job Bank – websites that cater to job seekers

MBTI – Myers Briggs Type Indicator

MD – managing director

MMDI – Mental Muscle Diagram Indicator

NDA – non-disclosure agreement

NSA – National Secretaries Association

NYCA – New York Celebrity Assistants

Old school – observant of traditional values

Org chart – organizational chart

PA – personal assistant

PCD – portable communication device

PPA – Plan, Prioritize, Action

Paralegal – a professional trained in legal matters to assist lawyers

RRSP – registered retirement savings plan

STAR – (situation/task, action and result) interview technique

Temp – temporary employee (secretary, assistant)

VIP – very important person

VP – vice president

VPA – vice president's assistant

WPM – words per minute

Select Resource List

1. Association of Administrative Assistants (AAA) – www.aaa.ca
2. Association of Secretaries and Administrative Professionals (ASAP) –www.asaporg.com
3. Executive Assistants Network of Canada (EANOC) – www.executiveassistants.ca
4. Exclusive job board for Administrative Professionals (Canada) – www.admincareerscanada.com
5. National and international salary surveys and pay scales – www.payscale.com
6. The International Association of Administrative Professionals (IAAP) – www.iaap-hq.org
7. The Elite Secretary. The Definitive Guide to a Successful Career – www.elitesecretary.com

Recommended Reading (My Top Ten for the Elite Secretary)

1. Axelrod, Alan. *My First Book of Business Etiquette*. Philadelphia: Quirk Books, 2004.
2. Devereux, G. R. M. *Etiquette for Men: A Book of Modern Manners and Customs*. London: Octopus Publishing, 2002.
3. Davison, Irene. *Etiquette for Women: A Book of Modern Manners and Customs*. London: Octopus Publishing, 2002.
4. Doyle, Michael, and David Strauss. *How to Make Meetings Work: The New Interactive Method*. New York: The Berkley Publishing Group, 1976.
5. Johnson, Spencer, MD. *Who Moved My Cheese?* New York: G.P. Putnam's Sons, 1998, 2002.
6. Klein, Eric, and John B. Izzo, PhD. *Awakening Corporate Soul: Four Paths to Unleash the Power of People at Work*. Lion's Bay: Fairwinds Press, 1998.
7. Levine, Stuart R. *Cut to the Chase: And 99 Other Rules to Liberate Yourself and Gain Back the Gift of Time*. New York: Doubleday, 2006.

8. Nurnberg, Maxwell, and Morris Rosenblum. *How to Build a Better Vocabulary.* New York: Warner Books, 1977.
9. Roetzel, Bernhard. *Gentleman: A Timeless Fashion.* Germany: Tandem Verlag GmbH – KONEMANN, 2004.
10. Zinsser, William K. *On Writing Well.* New York, NY. 1995

Recommended Television Shows and Movies

1. *The Good Wife.* CBS (USA). (TV Series 2009–).
2. *Mad Men.* AMC 2007 (USA) (TV Series 2007–).
3. *The Office.* BBC, UK (TV Series 2001–03).
4. *Working Girl.* 20th Century Fox (USA) (Movie 1988).
5. *The Devil Wears Prada.* 20th Century Fox (USA) (Movie 2006)

References

BBC Home. "PAs cast have "Secs" Appeal—dynamic young cast to star in BBC three-drama series." Press Release. Accessed December 11, 2008, http://www.bbc.co.uk/pressoffi ce/pressreleases/stories/2008/06_june/02/pas.shtml.

CNN Law Centre, with Rusty Dornin. "Two ex-Coke workers sentenced in Pepsi plot deal." *CNN.com,* accessed June 25, 2011,

http://www.cnn.com/2007/LAW/05/23/coca.cola.sentencing.

CNN Law Centre, with Rusty Dornin. "Coke requests court secrecy." *CNN.com,* Friday, July 7, 2006. Accessed September 11, 2007,

http://www.cnn.com/2006/LAW/07/06/coke.secrets.

"Court serves notice on the office bully." *The Times of London,* August 9, 2006. Accessed August 15, 2006, http://www.thetimes.co.uk/tto/career/article1793660.ece.

Daniel, Diann. "Five Keys to Getting (and Keeping) a Great Executive Assistant." *CIO Magazine*, April 25, 2007. Accessed September 9, 2010, http://www.cio.com/article/106103/Five_Keys_to_Getting_and_Keeping_a_Great_Executive_Assistant?page=1&taxonomyId=3123.

Davis, Evan. *The Bottom Line.* BBC Radio 4, June 23, 2011,

http://www.bbc.co.uk/programmes/b01206c6.

"The Disappearance of Ambrose Small – Case Closed." *Russianbooks.org.* Accessed October 16, 2005, http://www.russianbooks.org/small.htm.

Doran, George, Arthur Miller, and James Cunningham. "There's a SMART way to write management's goals and objectives." *Management Review* 70.11, 1981.

Drucker, Peter. Management by Objectives. "Defining objectives for employees and directing their performance against these objectives. Explanation of Management by Objectives of Peter Drucker ('54)." *SMART.* Accessed March 20, 2011, http://www.12manage.com/methods_smart_management_by_objecstives.html.

Egan, Gerard, with assistance from Richard F. McGourty and Hany Shamshoum. *Skilled Helping around the World*. Belmont, CA: Thomson Brooks/Cole, 2005.

Finder, Joseph. "About Men: A Male Secretary." *The New York Times*, February 22, 1987, www.nytimes.com/1987/02/22/magazine/about-men-a-male-secretary.htm.

Fresco, Adam. "£800,000 payout for bullied City secretary." *The Times*, August 1, 2006. Accessed August 3, 2006, http://www.thetimes.co.uk/tto/law/article2215353.ece.

"Secretary bullied in "department from Hell" is awarded £800,000." *The Times*, August 2, 2006. Accessed August 3, 2006, http://www.thetimes.co.uk/tto/career/article1793832.ece.

"Gender pay differentials examined." *Eurofound*. Accessed April 3, 2007, http://www.eurofound.europa.eu/eiro/2001/04/inbrief/it0104181n.html.

Gerard, Jasper. "Bullying court case led victim to lost family." *The Sunday Times*, August 6, 2006. Accessed August 15, 2006, http://www.thesundaytimes.co.uk/sto/news/uk_news/article159075.ece.

Gomez, Dominique. "For gender equality we need more male secretaries, like Obama's Jeremy Bernard." *Christian Science Monitor.* Accessed June 25, 2011, http://www.csmonitor.com/Commentary/Opion/2011/0228/

for-gender-equality-we-need-more-male-secretaries-like-obama-s-Jeremy-Bernard.

Gottlieb Wolfe Syosset, Marjorie. "Year-By-Year Chronology of the Secretarial Profession." Accessed April 3, 2007, http://www.crazycolour.com/os/secretary_01.shtml.

Hanson, Julie. "Five Keys to Getting and Keeping a Great Executive Assistant." *CIO Magazine,* April 15, 2004. Accessed September 9, 2010, http://www.cio.com/article/106103/Five_Keys_to_Getting_and_Keeping_a_GreatExecutive_Assistant?page=1&taxonomyId=3123.

Industry Canada. "Key Small Business Statistics – July 2006." Accessed March 15, 2010, http://www.ic.gc.ca/eic/site/sbrp-rppe.nsf/eng/rd02026.html.

The International Association of Administrative Professionals. "About: History." *IAAP.* Accessed January 8, 2007, http://www.iaap-hq.org/about/history.

"Administrative Professionals Week History: Name changed to Administrative Professionals Week." *IAAP.* Accessed September 5, 2010, http://www.iaap-hq.org/newsroom/apw/history.html.

"Isaac Pitman." *Answers.com.* Accessed June 25, 2011, http://www.answers.com/topic/isaac-pitman.

Kloess, Martin. "SMART Goals – A Key to Success." *All Voices.com.* Accessed March 25, 2011. http://allvoices.com/contributed-news/5507269-smart-goals-a-key-to-success.

Letter to the Editor. "Bullyboy tactics." *The Times of London*, August 8, 2006. Accessed August 15, 2006, http://www.thetimes.co.uk/tto/opinion/letters/article2068081.ece.

"Male Order. Male Secretaries not unusual in the Labour Party." *The Irish Times*, February 2, 1998. Accessed February 15, 2007, http://www.irishtimes.com/newspaper/weekend/1998/0214/98021400260.html.

"Male Administrative Assistant – and no, I'm not gay." *About My Job: Corporate America.* Accessed March 4, 2007, http://www.aboutmyjob.com/2045/male-administrative-assistant-and-no-im-not-gay/.

"MBTI Basics." *Myers Briggs.org.* Accessed March 14, 2010, http://www.myersbriggs.org/my-mbti-personality-type/mbti-basics.

McRae, David. "Employers must act to stop workplace bullies." *The Times*, August 2, 2006. Accessed August 15, 2006, http://www.thetimes.co.uk/tto/opinion/article2038712.ece.

Merryn on Money. "Sympathy for the £800,000 woman." *The Sunday Times*, August 13, 2006. Accessed August 15, 2006, http://www.thesundaytimes.co.uk/sto/business/money/article160368.ece.

"MMDI Questionnaire Report." Accessed March 24, 2010, http://www.teamtechnology.co.uk/mmdi/reportv2/.

"Myers-Briggs Widely Used but Still Controversial." *Psychometric-Success.com.* Accessed March 24, 2010,

http://www.psychometric-success.com/personality-tests/personality-tests-popular-tests.htm

New York Celebrity Assistants. "NYCA in the News," quote from *Vanity Fair. NYCA.com.* Accessed December 20, 2009, http://nycelebrityassistants.org/.

Pearsall, Judy, and Bill Trumble. *The Oxford English Reference Dictionary.* Oxford: Oxford University Press, 1996.

Paparella, Domencio. "Gender pay differentials examined." *Eurofound.* Accessed March 4, 2007, http://www.eurofound.europa.eu/eiro/2001/04/inbrief/it0104181n.html.

"Popular Tests." *Psychometric-success.com.* Accessed July 26, 2010, www.psychometric-success.com/personality-tests/popular-tests.htm.

"Reggie Love." *Wikipedia.* Accessed November 18, 2010, http://en.wikipedia.org/wiki/Regie_Love.

Sankey, Derek. "Administrative personnel taking on more responsibilities." *The Calgary Herald,* July 7, 2010. Accessed July 26, 2010, http://www.working.com.

"Secretary called 'bitch' and made to scrub male toilets wins damages." *The Telegraph.* Accessed January 19, 2010, http://www.telegraph.co.uk/news/uknews/4689236/Secretary-called-bitch-and-made-to-scrub-male-toilets-wins-damages.html.

"Super-skilled male secretary loses agency sex bias claim." *The Independent.* Accessed January 22, 2010, http://www.independent.co.uk/news/superskilled-male-secretary-loses-agency-sex-bias-claim-1324686.html.

Snowdon, Graham. "How do you rank on personal hygiene?" *The Guardian.* Accessed December 5, 2010, http://www.guardian.co.uk/money/blog/2010/sep/23/personal-hygiene-bad-habits?INTCMP=SRCH.

Statistics Canada. *The Daily Archives*, Tuesday, March 17, 1998. "1996 Census: Labour force activity, occupation and industry, place of work, mode of transportation to work, unpaid work." Accessed May 24, 2005, http://www.statcan.gc.ca/daily-quotidien/980317/dq980317-eng.htm.

Take a note … BBC Three appoints P.A.s, a new drama series from BBC Scotland, BBC.co.uk, December 12, 2007, accessed February 15, 2010, http://www.bbc.co.uk/print/pressoffice/pressreleases/stories/2007/12_december/13/pas.shtml.

"Two Ex-Coke Workers Sentenced in Pepsi Plot Deal," *CNN.com.* Accessed June 25, 2011, http://www.cnn.com/2007/LAW/05/23/coca.cola.sentencing

US Small Business Administration. "Frequently Asked Questions." SBA.gov. Accessed April 4, 2010, http://web.sba.gov.faqs/faqsindex.cfm?areaID=15.

Index

D

E

F

G

H

I

J

K

L

M

N

O

P

Q

R

S

T

U

V

W